**40**
*days in*

# THE
# PSALMS

# Titles in 40 Days Series

# 40
## *days in*

# THE
# PSALMS

## T. J. BETTS

*— edited by —*

## WILLIAM F. COOK III

PUBLISHING
NASHVILLE, TENNESSEE

# Contents

# Preface

Forty is an important number in the Bible. Moses was on Mount Sinai with the Lord God for forty days (Exod. 34:28), Elijah traveled for forty days before arriving at Mount Horeb (1 Kings 19:3–8), and Jesus was tempted in the wilderness for forty days (Mark 1:13). Some self-help experts believe it takes forty days to develop a habit. Whether they're right or wrong, there is no habit more important for a Christian to develop than a consistent devotional life.

In *40 Days in the Word*, readers will discover a humble attempt to assist believers longing for a fresh moving of God's Spirit in their life. This series intends to enable believers to read through books of the Bible in their devotional time discovering God's truth within its biblical context. The Spirit of God uses the Word of God to mature believers in their faith and increase their passion and zeal for Jesus Christ.

Many Christians find it difficult to sustain momentum in their devotional life. They desire to read the Bible consistently but lack encouragement, guidance, and direction. Commentaries are often too technical, and devotionals may fail to challenge them to dig deeply into God's Word. The *40 Days* series offers both a deeper discussion of a biblical passage and at the same time encourages the reader to make personal application based upon what the text *actually* says.

We live in a day where casual Christianity (which is not biblical Christianity at all!) has infected the church in the West. People are clamoring for shorter sermons that are more focused on felt-needs rather than on the Bible, and many in the pulpits are obliging. Furthermore, the songs that are often sung fail to extol the greatness of God, but instead make people feel better about themselves and their comfortable lifestyles.

If the church in the West is to recapture the passion of the early church, God's people must spend time on their knees with their Bibles open, allowing God's Spirit to convict them of their sin, build them up in their faith, and empower them to take the gospel across the street and around the world. The hope of the authors of this series is that God's Spirit will use these volumes to help God's people develop an ever-increasing love for their Savior, Jesus Christ.

In addition to helping individual believers, the series holds out hope for small groups desiring to focus their meetings on the study of the Bible. A group would spend approximately two months (five days of readings per week) reading through a book of the Bible along with the *40 Days* volume, and then base their discipleship time encouraging each other with what they discovered during the previous week.

The Spirit of God and the Word of God work together to strengthen God's church. The apostle Paul put it this way: "Let the word of Christ dwell richly among you, in all wisdom teaching and admonishing one another through psalms, hymns, and spiritual songs, singing to God with gratitude in your hearts" (Col. 3:16). Paul's hope is my prayer for you as you journey through these next forty days.

Bill Cook
Holy Week, 2020

# Two Ways

*Psalm 1*

## The Big Picture

Both Psalm 1 and Psalm 2 provide an introduction to the Psalms. Psalm 1 emphasizes how happily blessed is the individual who lives a godly life in commitment to God's Word. It is an invitation and exhortation to immerse oneself in the psalms by knowing and meditating on them because they provide instruction and perspective concerning every aspect of life. [These ultimately lead to a life that gives honor and joyful praise to God as depicted in Psalms 145–150. This happily blessed life contrasts with the meaningless lives of the ungodly who ultimately will perish. All must decide which path to take but must do so by recognizing that everyone will someday answer to God in the judgment.]

## Digging In

The first three verses of Psalm 1 describe the kind of person who lives a truly happy, joyful, blessed life. Such blessedness is more than mere emotion, but at the same time, it involves deep emotion and great satisfaction. These verses indicate this life is characterized by what one doesn't do (Ps. 1:1), by what one does do (1:2), and is naturally characterized by the abundant blessing resulting from this lifestyle described in the first two verses (1:3). What are the three things the happily blessed person does not do? ① The happily blessed person does not listen to the advice of unbelievers no matter how upstanding they may appear. ② The happily blessed person does not conform to the ways of those who live in disobedience and rebellion against God, and ③ the happily blessed person does not align with those outspoken individuals who derisively mock God and the people of God (1:1). Even if unbelievers appear to be morally good people and upstanding citizens, they know nothing of the things of God and have no desire to serve him. Their way of thinking is completely foreign to faith in God and a commitment to his Word. Regardless of how people with no faith in God conduct themselves, either quietly or loudly, the happily blessed person recognizes their inadequacies and rejects their godless influence.

Instead, the happily blessed person delights in God's Word and continually meditates on it (1:2). Meditation on God's Word requires first reading God's Word and then knowing God's Word. The Hebrew word for "meditates" literally means "to utter" the words with the sense of doing it repeatedly as one ponders its meaning. It might be likened to talking to oneself. Immersing oneself in God's Word shapes one's mind and then naturally shapes how one lives. But it is more than just an activity. This happily blessed life begins with delighting in God's Word because of one's delight in the Lord, the object of one's desire and affection. When one delights in something or somebody, one delights in that which pertains to them.

What does the person who lives this way look like? "He is like a tree planted beside flowing streams that bears its fruit in its season and its leaf does not wither. Whatever he does prospers" (1:3). The water is God's Word, strengthening the happily blessed person producing the fruit of righteousness. "Season" implies times of planting, times of growth, and times of harvest. It is the picture of taking in God's Word, allowing it to take root within, and finally seeing its fruit. It describes the ongoing, seasonal work of sanctification in a believer's life.

Moreover, his "leaf does not wither." The continual watering of God's Word will sustain the happily blessed person, resulting in a thriving life lived unto God; this is true prosperity. Such logic underpins one of the reasons this psalm brings to mind the Wisdom writings of the Old Testament, especially the book of Proverbs. Not only does it employ the motif of contrasting two ways of life, but when one orders one's life in such a way as to shun the way of the wicked and cling to the way of God's Word, the divinely ordered result established by the Creator will be abundance and joy. Proverbs 10:28 states, "The hope of the righteous is joy, but the expectation of the wicked will perish."

Consequently, Psalm 1:4–5 describe the wicked and what they should expect. They are nothing like those described above (1:4a). Those who reject the ways of unbelievers and immerse themselves in God's Word are firmly rooted. However, the wicked "are like chaff that the wind blows away." In ancient Israel, upon harvesting the wheat and barley, farmers brought their crops to the threshing floor to crush them and thereby separate the grain from the stalks. Once that was done, they winnowed the stalks. Winnowing involved waving or tossing the stalks into the wind so that the chaff, the inedible, useless covering of the grain, would blow away and the edible grain would fall to the ground. The wicked ultimately are both rootless and useless when it comes to spiritual matters. Psalm 127:1 states, "Unless the LORD builds the house, its builders labor over it in vain." Therefore, the wicked "will not stand up in the judgment" nor "in the assembly of the righteous" (1:5). We must live circumspectly, recognizing all of us one day will face God in the final judgment and give an account for our lives. On that day, God will separate the wicked from the righteous.

In conclusion, verse 6 indicates "the LORD watches over the way of the righteous." Literally, in its original language of Hebrew it reads the LORD "knows" the way of the righteous. This truth should give great comfort to believers. Such knowledge is an intimate relational knowledge God has for his children alone. It is both the evidence and security of our salvation. It is a wondrous thing to know the Lord, but just as wonderful is the truth that he knows us. The "righteous" are those who, like Abraham, have placed their faith in God and become his covenant people. On the other hand, "the way of the wicked leads to ruin." Their dreams, their plans, their way of life will come to ruin. All of it is meaningless apart from faith in God.

## Living It Out

There are two paths to living. One path leads to life and the other to death. The key to living a happily blessed life is by faith in God and by living for God, rejecting any influence that would detract one's commitment to him. It involves delighting in God's Word and being completely immersed in it, daily reading it, meditating upon it, and living one's life in accordance to it. It means looking to Christ, the only one to truly live in perfect obedience to God's law. Consequently, everyone will stand before God when the final judgment comes. The unbeliever must recognize life is meaningless apart from placing one's faith in the Lord and living for him. Otherwise, everything is temporary, ultimately meaningless, leading to ruin in the final judgment.

# The Wisdom of Worshiping the King

*Psalm 2*

## The Big Picture

As previously noted, Psalm 1 and Psalm 2 comprise the introduction to the book of Psalms; Psalm 1 begins with blessing, and Psalm 2 concludes with blessing. Together, both contrast the folly of rebelling against God with the wisdom of living one's life according to his Word and worshiping him. Psalm 1 shows the contrast at a personal level, and Psalm 2 shows it at the national level. Although Psalm 2 has no superscription, Acts 4:25 indicates it was written by David. Psalm 2 speaks of David while at the same time anticipating the coming Messiah, the Lord's anointed one who will rule the nations.

## Digging In

Psalm 2 is composed of four sections. The first section, verses 1–3, in consternation asks how the nations and their leaders all over the earth could rebel against the rule of the Lord and "his Anointed One."

The Hebrew word for "plot" in verse 1 is the same word for "meditates" in Psalm 1:2. The nations of 2:1 are consumed with freeing themselves from "their chains" and "restraints" they believe God has put on them. David's surprise comes from wondering how anyone could stand up to God and survive it (cf. 2:12a) and how anyone could feel enslaved by God when the one who takes refuge in him is "happy" (cf. 2:12b). It conveys the futility and irrationality of rebelling against God.

The expression, "anointed one," means "messiah" in Hebrew. The Greek of the New Testament translates the word *christos,* which in English is "Christ." David foreshadowed in a limited way what the Lord Jesus Christ would accomplish and be in an ultimate way. Therefore, Psalm 2 anticipates the person and work of the Lord Jesus Christ, and provides a description of our human inclination to rebel against the rule of God the Father and his Son. King Herod and Pontius Pilate along with most people in their kingdoms provide representative faces to this rebellion against the Lord.

The second section, verses 4–6, describes God's response to such foolishness. The King in heaven mocks them with laughter and ridicule because of the absurdity of their intentions. These temporary kings who rule nations with boundaries cannot succeed against the King who sits enthroned in heaven who eternally rules over all creation. This reality is clear when the Lord "speaks to them in his anger and terrifies them with his wrath." Emphatically, he declares "I have installed my king on Zion, my holy mountain" (2:6). The rulers of the earth have no rightful claim to authority within themselves. They are usurpers. But God has installed his king, the Lord Jesus Christ, who has complete authority and rules over the nations. It is for this reason, Jesus could say to his disciples, "All authority has been given to me in heaven and on earth" (Matt. 28:18). He will rule from Mount Zion. Mount Zion was the place where God chose to display his manifest presence to his people Israel when Solomon built the temple. Therefore, it is God's holy mountain, devoted to worship and the manifest presence of God on the earth.

In the third section, verses 7–9, the Anointed One speaks. He declares his legitimacy to rule based upon "the LORD's decree." In contrast to earthly rulers, the Anointed One had no need to assert himself to grasp the throne. Instead, God invested his enthronement upon him. He is the legitimate king because he is God's Son. When God established his covenant with David, promising David that David's house and kingdom will endure before God forever and that David's throne would be established forever, God stated concerning the king that "I will be his father, and he will be my son" (2 Sam. 7:13–16). This demonstrated the kind of relationship the kings in David's line could have with God. And the next phrase, which literally in Hebrew states "Today I have begotten you," accentuates the intimacy of this relationship.

However, there is only one descendant of David who fulfills this promise. Hebrews 1:5 indicates it is the Lord Jesus Christ, God's Son, but there's more. The Lord then told his Anointed One to "Ask of me, and I will make the nations your inheritance and the ends of the earth your possession." In whom is this realized? Hebrews 1:2 reveals "In these last days, he [God] has spoken to us by his Son. God has appointed him heir of all things." Consequently, as the king who inherits rule over every nation, the Anointed One—the Lord Jesus Christ, will "break" and "shatter" the rebellion against God and judge the nations (Rev. 2:27; 12:5; 19:15). In Matthew 25:31–46, Jesus describes how he will judge the nations. Some people "will go away into eternal punishment, but the righteous into eternal life" (Matt. 25:46).

Therefore, the fourth and final section, verses 10–12, serves as an exhortation and warning. It exhorts the kings and rulers of the earth to be wise and choose to receive instruction, to serve the Lord by worshiping and obeying him. This is the way to living a happily blessed life. Conversely, if the kings and rulers continue on their path of rebellion they will discover it is the path to their doom, for no one will be able to survive the wrath of the Anointed One who will uphold the honor of his heavenly Father. This warning may appear harsh, but in truth, it reveals a patient, merciful, and gracious God. Even though they deserved God's judgment of these rebellious leaders, he chooses to warn them and thus give them the opportunity to come to their senses and wisely choose to listen to instruction and experience a truly blessed life by taking refuge in the Lord.

## Living It Out

Psalm 2 highlights the foolishness of rebelling against God's authority over us. Because of our inherent sinful nature, we are predisposed to desire independence from God. We want to rule our own lives. But where does our self-rule get us? [Living independent of God's loving authority robs us of the happily blessed life which we were created to enjoy, and insubordination to God is the path to ultimate destruction.] The one who takes refuge in God by loving him and delighting in his Word will experience a happily blessed life.

# Turning to God in Times of Difficulty

*Psalms 3–4*

## The Big Picture

Psalms 3 and 4 are both psalms of David and prayers he prayed when oppressed by his enemies. The superscription of Psalm 3 indicates the circumstances of this prayer were when David was ousted from the throne of Israel by his son Absalom and was fleeing for his life (cf. 2 Sam. 15–16). It is reasonable to consider the night-time prayer of Psalm 4 was uttered during this period of his life too as David contemplated his perilous state of affairs. For instance, both psalms refer to lying down and sleeping, and both recognized the threat of David's enemies and the salvation, peace, and security belonging to the one who puts one's trust in the Lord. However, whether or not David prayed these psalms during the same crisis or on two completely separate occasions is ultimately irrelevant. Both prayers show the wisdom in turning to God in faith during times of difficulty and the help that comes from him.

## Digging In

The prayers of both Psalms 3 and 4 consist of a plea for God's help. David prayed, "Save me, my God!" (Ps. 3:7), "Answer me when I call," "be gracious to me and hear my prayer" (4:1), and "the LORD will hear when I call to him" (4:3). Such appeals and declarations are a display of true faith in God—faith that God graciously hears the prayers of his children, faith that he cares about his children, and faith that he is able to deliver them in their time of need. Children of God are never stronger than when they recognize their total dependence on God, and their situation is never more precarious than when they fail to recognize that dependence. Moreover, the strength that comes from this recognized dependency on God ushers in a confidence that chases away every fear.

Such confidence does not come from the foolish notion that "I believe it, therefore it must be so." No, it comes from the reality of who God is. He is a "shield around" those who put their trust in him (3:3). He answers the prayers of his servants (3:4) and "sustains" them, meaning they can lean on God for support (3:5). The people of God are in his favor and he delivers them from trouble (3:8). He is a righteous God who upholds his righteous people. In times past, God has freed his people when in a tight spot (4:1). It is this intimate knowledge of who God is that enables David to assert these claims and have confidence as he contemplates his present trouble. There are some things better forgotten, but the child of God must never forget God's faithfulness in the past. He is the same yesterday, today, and forever (Heb. 13:8). Remembering God's faithfulness in the past produces strength for present challenges and hope for the future.

Consequently, David denounced the attacks of his enemies, even when his enemies appeared to be a multitude and claimed God had abandoned him. David's declaration that his enemies love what is worthless and pursue lies most likely means that they were inventing false accusations against him to disgrace him. However, the words David spoke to himself were far more important than the words his enemies spoke about him. In Psalm 3:5–6 he wrote, "I lie down and sleep; I wake again because the LORD sustains me. I will not be afraid of thousands of people who have taken their stand against me on every side. David reminded himself of the rest and support that comes from trusting in the Lord. Therefore, no matter how desperate his situation appeared to be, he would not be afraid. He knew the God who had struck down and broken his enemies in the past would do so again (3:7).

In addition, in Psalm 4:3–5 David addressed himself saying, "Know that the LORD has set apart the faithful for himself; the LORD will hear when I call to him. Be angry and do not sin; on your bed, reflect in your heart and be still. Offer sacrifices in righteousness and trust in the LORD." Of what did David remind himself? 1) God sets apart the faithful from the unfaithful. God makes a distinction between those who love and serve him and those who do not. God takes sides, and he takes the side of those who are faithful to him. 2) The Lord listens to the prayers of his children. Just as loving parents are attentive to the cries of their children, God is even more attentive to the cries of his children. 3) Do not allow your anger to lead you to sin. One can be angry about sin, but the answer to sin is never to sin. 4) Consider your own heart and be at rest. You cannot control the hearts of others, but you can deal with what is in your own heart. 5) Worship the Lord in righteous obedience no matter what your difficulty is. And 6) trust in the Lord.

Suffering of any kind is difficult, but suffering caused by others who purposely intend to cause one harm is especially challenging. Whatever, the cause of one's troubles and no matter how dire things get, instead of asking the question "Who can show us anything good?" (4:6), one must remember "Salvation belongs to the LORD" and pray for his blessing upon his people (3:8). It is then that like David, one will experience overflowing joy, peaceful rest, and safety (4:7–8).

## Living It Out

Jesus clearly teaches that the world will hate his followers because the world hated him first (John 15:18–25). This truth is somewhat comforting, but it does not remove the sting from the attacks of our enemies. Psalms 3 and 4 show us what we need to do when we suffer such abuse. We need to cry out to God for help, trusting him to hear our prayers as a loving father hears the cries of his child. ② We need to remember God is a saving God. And ③ we need to remind ourselves of who we are in Christ, to pursue righteousness, and to rest joyfully in his watchful care.

# A Morning Prayer

*Psalm 5*

## The Big Picture

Waking up in the morning and contemplating the challenges ahead can be overwhelming, especially when one realizes the turmoil of yesterday is still a reality today. Psalm 5, a psalm of David, is a morning prayer he prayed when he woke up with a heavy sigh and longed for God's help as he contemplated another day of contending with the oppression of his enemies. The particular situation he was in is unknown, but whatever it was, David recognized his need for God's help. The omission of the details of his situation make it easier for believers facing a difficult day to apply the psalm. David's prayer became a song. Accompanied by flutes, it provides encouragement to the people of God as they wake up to similar mornings.

## Digging In

Psalm 5 consists of five sections. The first section, verses 1–3, reveals the emphatic nature of David's plea. The parallel of "consider my sighing" and "pay attention to the sound of my cry" stress David's sense of urgency. In the Old Testament, when something is stated twice, it is the writer's way of expressing emphasis, but when stated three times, it becomes an extreme emphasis. The parallelism in verses 1–2 demonstrates this. David's prayer begins with three parallel imperatives: 1) "listen to my words," 2) "consider my sighing," and 3) "pay attention to the sound of my cry." These three imperatives, one right after another, communicate the intensity with which David made his petition.

Furthermore, David used three different parallel expressions to address God as he began the prayer: "LORD," "my King," and "God." Taken together, David used these names of God to express to Yahweh, his King and God, that he is the only one to whom he cries out and is the only one he believes can answer his prayer. There is no other. It demonstrates the deep confidence David had in God in this extreme situation. The repetition of "in the morning" demonstrates that out of all the things he could have done to try to deal with his problem, the first thing he did was take it to God in prayer. David did so expectantly, knowing God would hear his voice and would answer his plea.

In the second section, verses 4–6, David reveals that the foundation of his petition was based upon the character of God. A good and loving God cannot tolerate any form of malevolence. The Lord hates evil and is opposed to the wicked. God will not tolerate even a moment of evil in his presence. Though they try, the boastful cannot stand up in rebellion against God and survive, and they certainly will be unable to stand firm before God in the final judgment. God's hatred of "evildoers" means he completely rejects them and their ways. Therefore, he will destroy these liars who seek to do violence. David was desperate and appealed to his good and just God who abhorred evil to defend him from the attacks of these wicked ones who were seeking to harm him.

It was his trust in this God that enabled David to pray what he did in the third section, verses 7–8. David experienced the *hesed,* the "faithful love," of Yahweh and, therefore, was able to go to the sanctuary and worship. The word *hesed* in Hebrew, is the most profound word in the Old Testament to describe God's love for his people with whom he entered into a covenant. It speaks of the most intimate, loving, and faithful relationship one can have with another. David's confidence to worship and pray was because God mercifully and graciously entered into this covenant relationship with David's people, Israel, and also individually with David as God's chosen king for Israel. He was accepted by God because of the *hesed* God had shown him.

Consequently, David worshiped the Lord in "reverential awe" of him. How could one like David experience such kindness from God without responding in worship and a desire for God to lead him to live righteously? Because of his "adversaries," David needed the Lord's guidance. It is often in the face of adversity we are most prone to lose our way.

The fourth section, verses 9–10, describes David's enemies and what David asked God to do to them. David mentions four characteristics of his enemies: (1) What they say is untrustworthy. (2) Their goal is to destroy. (3) What they say is meant to ruin others. And (4) they conceal their destructive intentions with words that falsely convey friendship and truth. Additionally, David made three requests to God concerning these enemies: (1) Declare their guilt. (2) Let them be brought down by their own schemes. And (3) drive them away. One must note the reason David made these requests to God: "for they rebel against you." Ultimately, their sin was not just against David, but against God, and it is this reason that truly validates David's requests.

In the fifth and final section, verses 11–12, David praises God for his faithfulness to bless and protect the righteous, those who take refuge in him. They are completely sheltered and shielded from harm. He exhorts every person who belongs to the community of faith to "shout for joy" and "boast about" him. Those who love God will praise him and make him known to others.

## Living It Out

There are several truths believers can glean from Psalm 5. First, when we face dire circumstances and the enemy appears to have the upper hand, we should first cast our anxieties upon the Lord. We can do this with full confidence because he is our God and we are his people. Second, remember that we can cast our cares on the Lord because of who he is. He loathes evil and faithfully loves his children.

Therefore, he will punish the wicked and save those who belong to him. Third, the Lord will guide us during times of trouble when our desire is to live obediently and be devoted to him. And fourth, as we trust in the Lord to help us, let us rejoice in him and make his goodness known to others.

# Praying for Mercy and Justice

*Psalms 6–7*

## The Big Picture

Psalm 6 is the first of seven psalms that Bible teachers often call "penitential psalms." These are Psalms 6, 32, 38, 51, 102, 130, and 143. The penitential psalms express sorrow for sin. Psalm 6 does not clarify the sin David committed or the circumstances surrounding it. Whatever the sin was, David appealed to God to stop disciplining him for having committed it. The psalm appears to indicate David's enemies were somehow involved in the matter, possibly attempting to take advantage of him in his weakened state.

However, it is possible, given its placement after Psalms 3–5 and before Psalm 7, David's sin may have been an errant response to his enemies. It would be consistent with his "self-talk" we saw in Psalm 4:4 when David counseled himself to "Be angry, and do not sin," given Psalm 7 is David's plea for God to deliver him and judge his enemies. Since Psalm 7 is David's appeal asking God to judge his enemies, the placement of Psalm 7 after Psalm 6 may serve both as corrective instruction countering David's unwise attempt to take matters into his own hands and as a warning to those who fail to trust God to vindicate them by dealing with their enemies. In Psalm 7, David is innocent of any wrong doing, perhaps evidence of God's forgiveness in response to his sorrow for his sin expressed in Psalm 6. Whatever the situation, Psalms 6 and 7 demonstrate God will discipline his children whom he loves and can be trusted to judge the wicked.

## Digging In

Psalm 6 begins with a plea for mercy from God and concludes with a statement of faith in God. David indicates the source of his difficulty was the Lord, himself, and the reason was God was disciplining him for some sin in David's life. The word *rebuke* is the word *yahkach* in Hebrew and may refer to a court setting where one is judged. However, it also denotes the wise correction and instruction of a loving father as in Proverbs 3:12 which states, "the LORD disciplines the one he loves, just as a father disciplines the son in whom he delights." Here, verse 1 emphasizes this loving discipline.

Nevertheless, the Lord's sanctifying discipline can still seem endless and be difficult to endure (see Heb. 12:7–11). David was physically, emotionally, and spiritually affected by his sin and the Lord's discipline. Consequently, recognizing his guilt and terrified of God's anger, David begged the Lord to be gracious and have mercy on him. This is the only plea that sinners have before God. David needed the physical, emotional, spiritual healing that only God could provide. David recognized the one who disciplined him was the only one who could and would rescue him from the consequences of his sin. Furthermore, David knew that the Lord would save him because of the Lord's *hesed*, his unwavering covenantal love for him.

Nevertheless, David's concern was not only for his own deliverance but also for the opportunity to boast in what the Lord has done by saving him. In verse 5, the "remembrance of" the Lord in parallel with thanking the Lord emphasizes David's desire to praise the Lord for what he has done. How could David proclaim God's faithfulness to his servant and praise the Lord before others if David were to perish?

David's prayer was based upon his faith in God's steadfast love and David's longing to praise him and declare the Lord is his salvation.

Verses 6 and 7 indicate how David's enemies intensified his suffering as he spent each night groaning and weeping in grief. Still, David was able to reject his enemies because the Lord has heard his weeping and cries for help. What's more, David confidently knew the Lord was accepting his prayer (see Ps. 34:15–18). Verses 9 and 10 accentuate the reversal that will take place: David will be saved and his enemies will be the ones who shake with terror and be disgraced.

Psalm 7 has six parts to it: ① David cries for deliverance from his enemies (vv. 1–2); ② David claims he is righteous (vv. 3–5); ③ David calls for God to vindicate him (vv. 6–8); ④ David characterizes God as righteous who saves the upright and judges those who fail to repent (vv. 9–13); ⑤ David comments on the ways of the wicked one and his ultimate demise (vv. 14–16); and ⑥ David concludes with thanks and praise to "the LORD Most High" (v. 17).

Psalm 7 begins with "LORD" or Yahweh, God's personal covenantal name, and concludes with "the LORD/Yahweh Most High." All that David requested is viable because of the gracious covenant Yahweh made with his people. Everything in life begins and ends with this truth for the people of God. Accordingly, since the Lord is righteous and judges righteously, he is a refuge for the righteous. He saves, vindicates, and establishes them. However, the Lord is at war with the unrepentant, and the evil ways of the wicked one becomes his own undoing. Those who seek righteousness will reap righteousness, but the one who conceives trouble will reap "his own violence . . . on top of his head." Consequently, David vows that he will thank the Lord for his righteousness and sing praises about him.

## Living It Out

Psalms 6 and 7 both emphasize the detrimental effects of sin on a person's life, even on the life of a believer. Loss is always the result of sin, either loss of eternal life for the unbeliever or the loss of intimacy and a sense of peace with God for the believer. God is so opposed to evil and so loving of his children that he will discipline his children to steer them away from evil and back to himself.[So, we must desire to hate our sin as much as God hates it, repent when we have sinned, and praise God even in the midst of his discipline if our desire is to grow into the image of Christ.]We must base our requests on the person and work of Jesus Christ, the gracious salvation we have in him and his faithfulness, and remember that he is worthy of our thanksgiving and praise, especially in the most difficult times of our lives.[Additionally, the believer needs to trust God to judge the wicked at the right time and in the most appropriate way.]

# Praise to the Creator

*Psalm 8*

## The Big Picture

Unlike other psalms, [Psalm 8 doesn't appear to refer to a particular situation in David's life] Instead, the song seems to be the outpouring of David's thoughts as he gazed into the night sky. As a shepherd, he surely had many occasions when he witnessed, with awe, the majesty and glory of God in the heavens. The meaning of the word *Gittith* in the heading is uncertain. It could refer to a type of musical instrument, to a Gittite song from the Philistine city of Gath, meaning "winepress," or perhaps to the occasion when the song was to be sung, such as during the harvest. The placement of Psalm 8 following the outpourings of anguish we have seen in Psalms 3–7 conveys [the truth that no matter how difficult our circumstances may be and how awesome God is, the majestic Creator of the universe is attentively mindful of us. Such truth calls us to praise and worship this magnificent God]

## Digging In

Psalm 8 begins with directly praising the Lord. It is the only psalm to address God alone in its entirety, and it begins and ends with the same refrain praising the Lord. David asserts that Yahweh—Israel's personal, covenantal God—is "our Lord," and not just the Lord of Israel, but the Lord over all humanity. Yahweh, the self-existing one, is our sovereign master and king, and his supremacy and dignity manifests itself throughout the earth. Enveloped between this refrain are two wondrous observations of Yahweh's dominion over all creation and Yahweh's consideration of humanity above the rest of creation.

In the last line of verse 1 and into verse 2, David proclaims Yahweh's dominion over all creation. The word *majesty* refers to Yahweh's regal glory, his royal splendor. It extols Yahweh's complete sovereignty and breathtaking omnipotence above his creation. It recognizes who the Lord is and what he has done on a grand scale. But in particular, what is just as amazing is how God uses the weak, "the mouths of infants and nursing babies," to demonstrate his strength and silence his enemies (1 Cor. 1:26–29). In fact, in Matthew 21:15–16, Jesus quoted this phrase to rebuke his enemies. The Lord Jesus Christ said that unless one becomes like a child one will never enter the kingdom of heaven (Matt. 18:4). The Lord himself is a stronghold for the needy and weak who cry out to him. Yahweh's display of his majestic splendor on behalf of his children terrifies their enemies (Isa. 30:30–33). The cries of those who trust in the Lord will be answered by a loving Father, resulting in the demise of the wicked and victory for his children.

Psalm 8 focuses most attention particularly on Yahweh's consideration of humanity over the rest of his creation. In verses 3 and 4, when David considers the vastness and wonders of the heavens and their starry hosts and the fact that God beautifully crafted them with his "fingers" and attentively set each one in its place. David is astonished how God could be mindful of human beings, who in comparison to the cosmos appear so insignificant. Why would the Creator of the universe be interested in puny humanity? Why does the Lord attentively listen to them when they call out to him and personally intervene on their behalf?

What is even more astounding is what Yahweh made humans to be. Verses 5–8 indicate God made human beings a "little less than God and crowned him with glory and honor." This phrase refers back to the time when God created human beings. First, God created them in his image. Second, God gave human beings the royal stewardship of ruling over his creation (Gen. 1:26–27). God's having put "everything under his feet" means God has given humanity dominion over all his creation (Gen. 1:28). The Lord elevated human beings and commissioned them to rule his creation under submission to God's rule. Hebrews 2:8 is a reminder that human sin has relinquished the fullness of this reality, but at the end of the age it will come to pass when all of creation submits to humanity's dominion over it as followers of Christ share in his rule (2 Tim. 2:12; Rev. 5:13).

When David reflects on all that God has done for humanity, he returns to the refrain he utters at the beginning of the psalm. Human beings may enjoy a lofty position in creation, but it is the Creator, Yahweh our sovereign Lord, who alone deserves all honor and glory. The high value human beings enjoy is based only on the truth that God values us and has undeservedly blessed us beyond measure. Consequently, the only right and appropriate response is to praise his name throughout the earth!

## Living It Out

Consider the heavens like David did. With present-day technology, there are about 10 billion galaxies in the observable universe containing about 1 billion trillion stars.[1] Nevertheless, as impressive as the universe God created is, nothing is more impressive than the kindness he has shown and continues to show humanity. He is mindful and attentive to our needs, taking delight in protecting and helping the weak. God created us in his image and gave us a position just below himself, crowning us with honor and glory, enabling us to share in his rule over creation. He created us to be like him. For this reason it is essential for us to look to Jesus Christ. He, alone, personifies what we were created to be and in him ultimately will be. The day is coming when we will see Jesus face to face and be made like him. Considering these truths, let us join in David's song of praise to our sovereign Lord.

## Day Seven

# God's Justice

*Psalms 9–10*

## The Big Picture

Psalms 9 and 10 focus on God's justice. [Psalm 9 begins with David's celebration of God's justice over the nations in the past but concludes with him praying that God would judge them in the present. Psalm 10, then, continues with this plea for God to judge the wicked but ends with a strong statement of faith that God will judge the nations and save the oppressed sometime in the future] For a number of convincing reasons, scholars believe these two psalms were originally one psalm that was later divided. For instance, Psalm 9 ends with "Selah," an expression that when it appears in other psalms is never at the end. Psalm 10 contains no heading which is unusual for this section of psalms, suggesting it is a continuation of Psalm 9. Also, when taken together, Psalms 9 and 10 form a broken acrostic. Several psalms begin each successive verse with a Hebrew letter of the alphabet to poetically communicate its comprehensiveness concerning the topic on which it focuses. [The broken acrostic of Psalms 9 and 10 probably is a poetic device conveying the brokenness of justice in the world] The two psalms were probably divided because Psalm 9 is mostly a celebration of God's justice while Psalm 10 is mostly a complaint about injustice.

Together, the message of Psalms 9 and 10 consists of 1) thanksgiving for God's acts of justice in the past, 2) a plea for God's rescue from the wicked in the present, and 3) a declaration of confidence in the Lord's deliverance from the wicked in the future with praise and thanksgiving.

## Digging In

[The first main idea these psalms convey is that believers have reason to voice thanksgiving and praise to God because he has shown himself faithful to protect his people by executing his righteous judgment on the wicked.] The four *"I will"* statements of Psalm 9:1–2 probably should be understood in the moment as opposed to being fulfilled sometime later in the future. The idea is more of a request asking God, "Let me thank the LORD with all my heart; let me declare all your wondrous works. Let me rejoice and boast about you; let me sing about your name, Most High." After these requests, David commences to do each in verses 3–16.

David declares that, as a righteous judge, God knows what is right, does what is right, and does it at the right time, in the right way, to the right extent. God puts things right (Ps. 9:4, 7–8). God has demonstrated his righteousness in the past by executing justice by rebuking and destroying the wicked (9:5–6, 15–16). The Lord has also demonstrated his righteousness by upholding the just cause of those who trust in him (9:4). He is the faithful refuge of those who seek him and will not forget the cry of the oppressed (9:9–12).

[The second main idea is based on God's demonstrated righteousness and faithfulness to deliver his people in the past. David is sure he can trust God to hear his cry and save him from his enemies in the present.] In the thick of the enemies' onslaughts, Yahweh seems distant and unobservable (10:1), not only for David but for his enemies (10:4–5, 11, 13). Because God appears to have abandoned the righteous, to be nonexistent and consequently no threat to the wicked, they are: arrogant, scheming, greedy, without accountability, scoffing, self-confident, hostile, cursing, deceitful, lurking, violent, malicious, oppressive, stealing, exploiting, and victimizing. Accordingly, the righteous are in dire straits. David's apparent complaint is an expression of faith. The fact that he is taking the matter to the Lord demonstrates that he trusts the Lord even though from his perspective he cannot see what the Lord is doing.

[This cry for relief is grounded upon two things David is sure of: 1) God's character to protect the helpless and 2) God's glory.]In Psalm 10:14, David says, "The helpless one entrusts himself to you; you are a helper of the fatherless." In Israelite society, fathers and husbands were the protectors and providers for their families. To be fatherless meant being so vulnerable that one's very life was in peril with no means to provide for or protect oneself. But God will not forget the oppressed or the fatherless. He knows what is happening; Yahweh will be their provision and protector.

But David's greatest concern was God's glory. With the wicked prospering, they denounce the existence of God, and believers begin to doubt God. Recalling Psalm 8 and speaking of the wicked, who are these "mere humans" in comparison to Yahweh? Let those who have despised God cringe in terror before Yahweh and stand in judgment before the awesome God of the nations (9:19–20). David prays for God to put an end to the wicked once and for all (10:15).

[Therefore, David's final point is that the people of God confidently can trust in their eternal King to save them, knowing the wicked will one day perish.]The future for believers is sure because Yahweh carefully listens to the desires of his people, will strengthen their hearts, and do right by them. Some day they will never experience the terrors brought on by mere humans ever again (10:16–18).

## Living It Out

David reminds us of an axiom every believer must remember: "Never forget in the darkness what God has shown you to be true in the light." Like David, when we experience times in our lives when it is difficult to see God or understand what he is doing, or in some instances, what he appears to not be doing, we must remember what God has done in the past. The One who has saved us and has shown himself to be faithful to his children in the past is still faithful to his children today and forevermore. So, we can praise God in our present circumstances and even in whatever our future circumstances may be because our Lord and Savior, Jesus Christ, has been crowned "King forever and ever" and will "strengthen" our "hearts." Believers are eternally secure in him.

# Keep the Faith

*Psalms 11–12*

## The Big Picture

[Psalms 11 and 12 are both psalms crying out to God for deliverance and fit well with the preceding context of Psalms 3 through 10.] It is difficult to know in what particular circumstance David was in when he wrote Psalms 11 and 12, and their focus within the context of laments, pleadings for God's help, is a little different from the other psalms. In these two psalms David not only focuses on the wicked as he has in preceding psalms but also on those who may have been his so-called friends and the effect they had on him during his time of difficulty. In Psalm 11, they suggest that the only thing the righteous can do when oppressed by the wicked is run away, and in Psalm 12, they apparently took their own advice and fled themselves. [Psalms 11 and 12 promote faith in Yahweh: have faith in Yahweh when tempted to lose faith, and have faith in his Word when all others appear to have lost their faith and abandon you.]

## Digging In

[Psalm 11 begins with David's declaration of faith in Yahweh in response to the advice he received to run away from the threats of the wicked (v. 1)] David's statement is emphatic. In Hebrew, the normal construction would be like English: "I have taken refuge in the Lord," subject–verb–object. But in Hebrew, a way of expressing something emphatically is to put the object first, so here it is literally object-subject-verb: "In the Lord, I have taken refuge!" David's emphasis was on Yahweh. Consequently, his response to the suggestion to flee was one of consternation. Their suggestion made no sense. There is no safer refuge than the Lord himself in times of trouble.

Nevertheless, when one's focus is off of Yahweh and focused on the threat instead, one is sure to lose hope. The wicked were armed and ready to attack from the shadows (v. 2). The idea is that the attack could come suddenly at any moment from any direction. The situation was grim and seemingly indefensible, and fleeing to the mountains like a bird made sense. Verse 2 also reveals that this attack was focused on "the upright in heart." To be upright literally means to be straight, the opposite of crooked. The wicked, those who are crooked, were set to attack the straight, the upright in heart who trusted and served Yahweh.

With all this description of the situation, David's declaration at the beginning of the psalm, is in response to the pessimistic and defeatist question voiced in verse 3: "When the foundations are destroyed, what can the righteous do?" In other words, they were asking, "When worldliness and lawlessness run amok and every foundation for righteousness in society has been thrown down, what can good people do?" The implied answer is that they can do nothing but run away.[But because their focus was on the trouble and not on Yahweh that they arrived to this wrong conclusion. David gave them the correct answer: take "refuge in the Lord!" He is the only sure foundation.]

In verses 4–7, David provides logical reasons for trusting in the Lord. 1) Yahweh reigns over all and sees everything that happens (v. 4). He is intimately aware of what every person is doing, and he is not shaken by any of it. 2) Yahweh examines or tests the righteous (v. 5a). He is especially interested in how the righteous respond to difficulties.

Will they respond in faith or despair? 3) <u>Yahweh completely rejects the</u> <u>wicked</u>. Fire connotes complete destruction. So, God will ultimately put an end to evil, and so David poetically prayed what he knew to be the will of God (vv. 5b–6). 4) Yahweh is righteous, so one can expect him to do what is right. <u>And 5) the upright will see Yahweh act on</u> <u>their behalf, but more importantly some day they will see his face (v. 7)</u>.

Psalm 12 has a simple A-B-A or chiastic pattern. The <u>first</u> section hyperbolically states no one remains who is faithful to the Lord (vv. 1–4). The <u>second</u> section shows that in a world where others are untrustworthy, one can always trust in the Word of God (vv. 5–7). And the <u>third</u> section returns to describing the wickedness of the human race (v. 8). When employing this A-B-A or chiastic structure, the writer is emphasizing the message of the central section. One can think of it as "the central idea" or "the heart of the matter." [Therefore, David's central message in Psalm 12 is that when the majority have become unfaithful to the Lord, continue to trust in God's Word]

The psalm begins with a cry for help because it appears the upright in heart have disappeared. Verses 1–4 describe the disloyalty of the human race. They are deceptive flatterers using manipulative words to their own sordid ends. They are proud of their ability to exploit others with their persuasive words. But David emphatically states their words are empty (v. 2a). Nevertheless, verse 5a describes the effects of these words causing "the devastation of the needy and the groaning of the poor." It is for this reason that David indignantly prayed that the deceivers would be "cut off," meaning removed or destroyed (v. 3). [In its conclusion, Psalm 12 reiterates the activities of the wicked as they exalt that which is worthless, meaning that which is vile and shameful]

[Where does one find hope in such a godless society? In the Word of God. In verse 5b, Yahweh says he will rise up and save those who long for God, taking action on their behalf] Then David states how trustworthy God's Word is in contrast to the empty words of the flatterers mentioned above. God's Word is completely "pure," without any imperfection (v. 6). In the Bible, the number seven often denotes completion and perfection. Here, David is saying God's Word is perfect in every way. And since God's Word is perfect, David knows he can trust it. Therefore, he is able to assert that God will keep and protect his people forever (v. 7). <u>David knows so because God's Word says so.</u>

## Living It Out

Keeping the faith can be difficult when much of what we see is increasing moral decay and decreasing faithfulness to the Lord. Our perspective can easily become skewed. It is for this reason we must not underestimate the importance of the daily intake and meditation of the Word of God. Instead of listening to the empty lies of this world, we desperately need the perfect Word of God to remind us of the truth. Jesus said, "I have told you these things so that in me you may have peace. You will have suffering in this world. Be courageous! I have conquered the world" (John 16:33).

# When God Is Silent

*Psalm 13*

## The Big Picture

Psalm 13 is a lament. Over one third of the psalms are psalms of lament. In the psalms of lament, the psalmists cries out to God in anguish. They usually include a description of their suffering and their grim circumstances, ask God to intervene and save them, and then either praise the Lord or promise to praise the Lord. Some of these laments are personal, and others of them are corporate, voiced for the people of God. Psalm 13 is a personal lament. Information revealing the precise occasion when David uttered this psalm is absent, but there are numerous times in David's life when David was in tremendous distress and it would have been fitting for him to have prayed this prayer. Because most of life is accompanied by either physical, emotional, or relational pain, the simple three-part structure of Psalm 13 carries a potent message for everyone. In the first section, verses 1–2, David questioned God. In the second section, verses 3–4, David voiced his request to God. And in the third and final section, verses 5–6, David declares his trust in God and promises to rejoice in the Lord's salvation.

## Digging In

David begins the psalm with four potent questions in verses 1–2, each beginning with the words "How long?" This expression reveals that the ordeal David is experiencing has been going on for quite some time. It also displays the frustration David has with God for not intervening on David's behalf. The first question reveals his sense of abandonment by God. David was aware of the promises God made to be with his people and act on their behalf. For God to "forget" David is a way of saying God has taken no action on David's behalf. From David's perspective, without God's intervention it seems as if there will be no end to this situation. The second question reveals the intensity of David's sense of trauma as he asks, "How long will you hide your face from me?" The idea of God's hiding his face from his people in the Old Testament is another way of expressing God's abandonment. It describes God's withholding his protection and blessing from his people as an act of discipline or judgment (Deut. 31:17; Ps. 27:9). On the contrary, when the Lord shines his face on his people it is a sign of blessing and sustenance for them (Num. 6:24–26; Ps. 67:1; Dan. 9:17).

With the third question, David asks how long must he be left to his own devices to resolve the matter? How can he acknowledge the Lord in all his ways if the Lord offers him no counsel? One plan after another fails, and every day the anguish is continually eating him up inside. He can find no answer for overcoming his enemies or reason for God's abandonment. David's fourth and final question is "How long will my enemies dominate me?" In Hebrew, the word translated "dominate" literally means "to be exalted" or "lifted up." As if his suffering already has not been enough, David sees his enemies rising to places of power and prominence and using their positions to persecute him. David was personally distraught because Yahweh, David's intimate loving God, had allowed all of this to go on.

It is with these burdens that David cries out to Yahweh, his God, for help (vv. 3–4). His prayer is straight to the point: 1) he asks God to "consider" him, and 2) he asks God to "answer" him (v. 3a). David is asking God to look at him intently and with favor, and therefore to answer him. His only hope is in the Lord to brighten his outlook and give him a proper perspective. If the Lord does not restore him, he feels like he will surely die. Instead of God or David having the last word, David's enemies will have it. They will gloat about their victory over the Lord's servant. And it will not only be a victory over David, it will also bring a reproach to the God of David. David's demise would show that his faith in Yahweh profited him nothing. It is not only David's honor at stake but also the Lord's.

Nevertheless, no matter how discouraged and disorientated David is in his crisis, he remembers he has put his trust in the Lord's *hesed*, Yahweh's faithful covenantal love (v. 5). One's trust can only be as strong as the object of that trust. Recognizing there is nothing greater to trust in than Yahweh's faithful love, David is able to rejoice in the Lord's deliverance. Because he knows the Lord, David trusts he will be able to sing to him since in times past he has treated him "generously" (v. 6). David's enemies will not be the ones rejoicing. His faith in Yahweh is so strong that David knows Yahweh will save him, and David also knows that he will be the one praising Yahweh when he does.

## Living It Out

It is difficult when the Lord appears to be ignoring our problems and prayers. It is even more difficult to understand why it happens. At times God will use silence to help us grow spiritually. It's possible that God wants to get our attention and realize, like David, that we are incapable of solving our troubles apart from him. Maybe there is unconfessed sin in our lives that we need to repent of. Or, perhaps God is testing our faith so that like David we will come out of the difficulty with a deeper commitment to him and greater desire to praise him. One thing is sure. God wants us to do what David did: seek the Lord with all of our heart, mind, soul, and strength. We must recognize what David knew—that those who seek the Lord and put their trust in him will not be disappointed.

# The Ungodly and the Godly

*Psalms 14–15*

## The Big Picture

[Psalms 14 and 15 provide a contrast between the ungodly and the godly. Psalm 14 describes the universal foolishness of humanity's denial of God and their futile attempts to thwart those who are righteous] The arrogant independence of the ungodly will be turned to dread when they realize God is against them.[On the contrary, Psalm 15 describes those who are accepted by the Lord, providing ten characteristics of the godly] Similar to Psalm 1, taken together, Psalms 14 and 15 describe the stark difference between the wicked and the righteous.

## Digging In

Psalm 14 contains three sections. The first section describes the foolish way of the ungodly (vv. 1–3). The second section pronounces the judgment that awaits the ungodly (vv. 4–6). And in the third section,

David voices his hope in God's salvation and restoration of the people of God (v. 7).

The description of the ungodly in verses 1–3 is revealing. At their core, they deny the very existence of God. It may not be with an outright declaration of atheism, but it most certainly is a practical atheism, living as if there is no God. This is the definition of being a fool. The book of Proverbs clearly teaches that wisdom is living all of life unto God, acknowledging him in everything. The fool is the opposite. He takes his own counsel and lives for himself, decidedly refusing to live his life according to the design of his Creator. The result of living a life that ignores God or outright denies God is corruption and "vile deeds." The fool is "corrupt" literally means that he is deliberately ruined. His "vile deeds" means his lifestyle is utterly disgusting, abominable to God.

The Lord inspects the human race, literally "the descendants of Adam." This expression hearkens back to Genesis when God looked down at the wickedness of the human race before the flood (Gen. 6:5) and looked down at humanity's grasp for fame with the Tower of Babel (Gen. 11:5). In all three instances, God looks "down" upon the human race, reminding the reader that God reigns over all creation. In this instance, God looks down to see if there is anyone who is wise. Here, David defines what it means to be wise: the one who seeks God is wise (Ps. 14:2). However, what God sees when he examines the human race is foolishness because all have turned away from God and have become corrupt. He sees no one who is good because there is no good apart from God. No deed, no matter how good it may appear, is good at all if it is done in selfish disregard to God.

Rom 1

[Verses 4–6 indicate the ungodly fail to understand because they have no capacity to do so without a knowledge of God.]Their ignorance is the result of their willful rejection of Yahweh. Eating bread was part of their everyday way of life for the people of that day. So, David says it is as natural for the ungodly to exploit the godly as it is for them to eat bread, while at the same time they ignore the only One who could satisfy their deepest needs. Consequently, the ungodly will one day be filled with dread when they realize the grave mistake they have made. [The same Lord who has intervened on behalf of his people in the past will surely do so over and over again until he has done it once and for all at the end of the age.]

Therefore, David concludes this prayer petitioning the Lord in Zion, Jerusalem, the place of his manifest presence and rule with his people, the place where his people are to gather together to worship him (Ps. 9:11). David asks the Lord to bring about the great salvation of his people and restore them, vindicate them and make things right (14:7).

While Psalm 14 describes the ungodly, those who reject Yahweh and are rejected by Yahweh, Psalm 15 provides ten characteristics of those who are godly, acceptable to God, and permitted to approach the Lord to worship him in his sanctuary. So, who is godly? 1) "The one who lives blamelessly." Noah, Abraham, and Job are all called "blameless" (Gen. 6:8; 17:1; Job 1:1).[It means having integrity toward God and others, seeking God's will for one's life.] 2) The one who "practices righteousness." To practice righteousness is to do what is right according to God's Word. 3) The one who "acknowledges the truth in his heart." It means being sincere by embracing the truth within and speaking the truth to others. 4) The one "who does not slander with his tongue." Slander is communicating with the intent to do harm to another. 5) The one "who does not harm his friend." It speaks of being a faithful friend. 6) The one who does not "discredit his neighbor." It involves abstaining from shaming one's neighbors when they are down. The opposite would be to honor them. 7) The one who has discernment, shunning those wicked who are rejected by the Lord and holding dear those who live for him. 8) The one "who keeps his word whatever the cost." It means not breaking a promise when it becomes difficult or inconvenient to keep it. 9) The one who does not lend money with interest. It means helping people in need without adding to their difficulty by charging them interest. It means lending aid to people in need without expecting anything in return. 10) The one who will not "take a bribe against the innocent." It means justice must be upheld with integrity at all times, abstaining from taking advantage of someone for personal gain.

God's Word promises those who bear these characteristics stand on a firm foundation in life and before God (v. 5c). Not only can they confidently approach God's throne, they also can rest assured God is with them.

## Living It Out

Together, Psalms 14 and 15 contrast those who live for themselves with those who live for the Lord. They teach us that one who is a practical atheist, living life as if God does not exist, is building one's life on a shaky foundation that ultimately will crumble. And these psalms amplify the truth that wisdom and success in life will be realized only in the life of the one who seeks the Lord and lives for him. Jesus said, "You can do nothing without me" (John 15:5). Apart from Christ our lives would be in ruin. However, God's Word also states we are "able to do all things through him who strengthens" us (Phil. 4:13). Let us shun what is evil, live for the Lord in all of life, and trust in him to make us more like Christ.

## Day Eleven

# The Believer's Protector

*Psalms 16–17*

## The Big Picture

In Psalms 16 and 17, David prays for the Lord to protect him from his enemies. The word *Miktam* occurs in the heading of Psalm 16 and Psalms 56–60, but its meaning is uncertain. It may be a musical term. Regardless, Psalm 16 emphasizes David's confidence in and worship of his good God whom David trusts to protect him, while Psalm 17 focuses more on his immediate situation as David is surrounded by his enemies who are poised to ambush him. Like several others previously, these psalms do not reveal the situation David was in. Nevertheless, the two psalms together reveal that God can be trusted to be good in all situations and therefore show believers the kind of committed confidence they may have in the Lord in the midst of severe trials.

41

## Digging In

Psalm 16 may be understood to have two sections easily memorable by alliteration. Verses 1–4 contain David's prayer for God's protection, and verses 5–11 reveal David's peace in God's protection. The psalm begins with David's initial plea for God to protect him in verse 1, but his mind moves quickly away from thinking about his difficulty to focusing on his God to whom he prays. We saw in Psalm 14:6, David said Yahweh is the refuge for the righteous. As a committed man of faith in the Lord, David could place his confidence in Yahweh, who over and over again had shown himself to be a trustworthy refuge. A refuge is the picture of a mother bird providing protection under her outstretched wings for her babies (Ps. 57:1; 61:4; 91:4) or that of a strong shield in battle (Prov. 30:5).

In Psalm 16:2, David highlights the intimate relationship he has with Yahweh, God's personal covenant name to his people. David declares Yahweh is his Lord, his master, and that all goodness resides in him. There is nothing good apart from Yahweh and doing what is good for his people is not beyond his character or ability. What's more, the one who is committed to God takes delight in the people of God (v. 3). Believers are a noble people because they are the Lord's inheritance (Isa. 19:25) and children of God (Gal. 3:26; 4:27; Rom. 8:14). Those who are faithful to the Lord are contrasted with those who worship other gods, those who should expect multiplied sorrows in their future. But David is committed to Yahweh, and even though many people around him have turned away from the Lord to worship false gods, David will not. He will not worship these false gods nor pray to them (v. 4).

Therefore, David is at peace because he recognizes the goodness of God. Saying Yahweh is his "portion" and "cup of blessing" means the Lord himself is everything David could ever truly desire or need. Everything he has and experiences in life is a blessing because of Yahweh. So, David's future is secure because the Lord holds his future (v. 5). Everything he has as his inheritance from the Lord is perfect. It is all he could ever hope for and more. David recognizes they are expressions of God's love for him (v. 6). David is at peace even at night when thoughts "trouble" him because the Lord quiets his mind as he meditates on the Lord (v. 7). David always put the Lord in front of him to lead him, and because the Lord holds his hand, David will not be "shaken" by difficulties (v. 8). Instead, he rejoices and rests secure in the Lord (v. 9). David knows that the God who has chosen him, loved him, provided for him, protected him and will not abandon him, even in death (v. 10). In the Lord's presence, we find immeasurable joy, and David trusts in the Lord's eternal faithfulness to believers because the Lord is the path to abundant and eternal life (v. 11).

Psalm 17 has a straightforward structure. Verses 1–5 contain David's appeal for justice based on his righteousness, verses 6–12 are an appeal for justice based on the enemy's wickedness, and even though the entire psalm speaks of God's justice, verses 13–15 is an emphatic appeal for God to act in accordance to his justice.

David begins the psalm desperately arguing that it would be right for God to help him because God knows he is innocent. Verses 1–5 indicate he is the kind of man we saw described in Psalm 15 whose worship is acceptable to God. The Lord should answer his prayer because the Lord has tested and examined his heart and knows he is a righteous man. His words and actions are those of a faithful servant of the Lord. He is a man of integrity. His life proves his cause is just, so it is logical for the God who upholds justice to hear his cry and intervene for his cause.

Therefore, David confidently calls on God because he knows he will answer his prayer. The word *listen* in Hebrew carries the idea of "hear and act." David is asking the Lord to act in a wondrous way, in such a way that when others see it they will know it was God who did it. For what is more wondrous than the gracious choosing of Israel to be his people and for him to be their God? Such a God is a saving God, and he saves those who seek refuge in him from those who rebel against him (v. 7). As his refuge, David knows God will protect him as one would protect one's eye or a mother bird would protect her babies even though the threat is imminent and deadly (vv. 8–9). It would be just for God to deal with David's enemies because God is against everything they are. They are arrogant; God is opposed to the proud. They are enemies of the righteous; God upholds the righteous. They are violent; God is the Prince of Peace.

So, David calls upon Yahweh to rise up, confront the wicked, and bring them down and save him (v. 13). David asks God to destroy those who live for the world and their own selfish desires, to "fill their bellies" with the judgment God has in store for them, to judge them as the just God that he is (v. 14). But as for David, he confidently knows he will see God's face in righteousness. Unlike the wicked, he will wake up every day with the satisfaction of knowing God is with him (v. 15). The word *presence* literally means "form" or "image." David's hope for the future gives him strength in the present.

## Living It Out

Several truths are highlighted in these psalms. It is a blessing to God and uplifting to believers to recognize and give thanks for God's goodness in all situations. When we remember the goodness of God and all that he has done, we are able to experience the peace of God. Also, the person who delights in the Lord will delight in his people, the church. One cannot truly love Jesus and not love what he loves. Next, the Lord delights in listening to our prayers and intervening on our behalf when our lives are totally devoted to him in joyful, loving obedience. Finally, as believers, we have the joy of looking to Christ for righteousness today and in the future someday to fall asleep only to wake up and be made perfectly like him.

# Praise for Deliverance

*Psalm 18*

## The Big Picture

Psalm 18 is a song of thanksgiving for the numerous victories God gave to David over his enemies including Saul. A parallel version of this song is recorded in 2 Samuel 22. [The psalm is divided into five sections: David's praise for Yahweh, his rock (vv. 1–3); a description of how Yahweh saved David (vv. 4–19); Yahweh's faithfulness to the righteous (vv. 20–29); a description of how God gives David his victories (vv. 30–45); and a return to David thanking and praising Yahweh, his rock (vv. 46–50).] Psalm 18 is the longest psalm so far, and it contains a number of elements we have observed in the previous laments or cries for deliverance. This psalm recognizes what Yahweh has done and praises Yahweh for having intervened and delivered David when David called out to him. David proclaims in verse 3: "I called to the LORD, who is worthy of praise, and I was saved from my enemies."

## Digging In

[David begins the psalm in a unique way stating, "I love you, LORD." Surprisingly, this is the only place this phrase may be found in the Old Testament, and Peter is the only one to address Jesus with these words in the New Testament (John 21:15–17). The word here, translated from Hebrew to English as "love," normally denotes God's love and compassion for his people and is often associated with the loving care of a mother for her children. Here it speaks of the intimate relationship David has with the Lord who is his strength, his rock, his fortress, his deliverer, his God, his refuge, his shield, his horn of salvation (possibly the horns on the altar representing a place of refuge), and his stronghold. David concludes his introduction stating the premise of his song of thanks: he called to the Lord, and the Lord saved him. And as the psalm reveals, Yahweh saved David numerous times.

The following section describes how Yahweh saved David (Ps. 18:4–19). David's circumstances were so dire he thought he was going to die. His description is similar to Jonah's when he was near death in the belly of the fish and cried to the Lord in his distress (Jonah 2:2–5). David cried to the Lord because he knew the Lord would help him. Next, David employs highly poetic language describing how God displayed his awesome power as he intervened on David's behalf and delivered him from his enemies (Ps. 18:7–15). Such manifestations of God in creation are called theophanies. In this instance, it is a picture of the Creator using his magnificent creation to wage war on behalf of his servant. David was in "deep water," but the Lord rescued him. David was in a tight spot, but Yahweh brought him out to "a spacious place." The enemy was too strong for David but was no match for Yahweh, and Yahweh did all of this for David because the Lord delights in his children (vv. 16–19).

Because the Lord is righteous, he is faithful to help those who are righteous, and it is for this reason he saved David. When David claims to be righteous and to have clean hands, he is not saying he has never sinned. David is expressing that God has forgiven him of his sin and declared him righteous on account of his faith and devotion to God. Righteousness is evidenced in the life of one who clings to God's Word and shuns sin (vv. 20–24). Salvation is by God's grace through faith alone, but God rewards his children when they are faithful to him. However, the Lord is just as faithful to deal justly and shrewdly with the wicked, turning their own twisted ways back on them (vv. 25–27). What a difference it makes when God illuminates David's dark thoughts of defeat and hopelessness expressed in previous psalms. Now, David is emboldened to take the offensive because Yahweh's light gives him a clear perspective and guidance to zealously overcome the enemy. With God's leadership David can confidently overcome any barrier the enemy lays before him (vv. 27–29).

Verses 30–45 describe how God gives David his victories. History demonstrates that great victories in battle are won by great strategists who know the perfect way to victory. David wins his victories because he looks to God. God's way is perfect and his Word is without any defect. David safely follows behind the Lord his shield (v. 30). Every aspect of David's victories are realized because of what God does for him. What does God do? God is his rock, providing David a firm foundation. He makes David strong. God makes David flawless and effective in battle. He gives David the ability to be fast and surefooted in order to get the most advantageous position in battle. God makes David so strong he can use the most difficult weapons with ease. God protects him and sustains him. God's gracious condescension to intervene on David's behalf is what makes David invincible. God gives him the space he needs to fight. God enables David to defeat his enemies, to bring them into submission, to cause them to flee before him and grovel beneath him. God empowers David to completely silence his enemies and bring them under David's rule. And in all of this, David gives God all the credit and all the glory.

David concludes his victory song where he begins it, declaring Yahweh is his rock and the God of his salvation. Then, couched in praise, David summarizes the points he makes in the song. God frees him from his enemies and enables David to defeat them, subdue them, and ultimately reign over them. God's intervention provides David the opportunity to give thanks and sing about the Lord as a witness to who is the one and only God, Yahweh. God gives great victories to David because God is loyal to his anointed and to his descendants (vv. 46–50).

This declaration anticipates the Anointed One and Son of David, the Lord Jesus Christ, who will one day defeat his enemies, subdue them, and save his people for eternity.

## Living It Out

Psalm 18 reminds us that just as David had his enemies, believers today do also. The New Testament indicates the world, the flesh, and the devil, along with death, are our enemies. This psalm also reminds us that the Lord has given us everything we need in himself to defeat these enemies. When Jesus was born, lived, died, was buried, rose again and ascended to his heavenly Father, he won the victory for us and through faith in him has saved us. He has filled us with the Holy Spirit and equipped us with his everything we need to resist our enemies. Everything God did for David he does for us in the person and work of the Lord Jesus Christ. We live and stand firm because of our victory in Jesus. So, let us trust in the Savior and praise him with thanksgiving just as David did.

## Day Thirteen

# God Reveals Himself through His Creation and Instruction

*Psalm 19*

### The Big Picture

In Psalm 19, David contemplates how creation proclaims the glory of God and then considers the riches of the Lord's instruction in the Scriptures. He recognizes that, unlike the gods of the nations who are aloof and silent, Yahweh is a God who graciously makes himself known through the revelation of creation (vv. 1–6) and the revelation of his Word (vv. 7–11). David understands that just as all of physical life is dependent on the sun, one's spiritual life is dependent on the Word of God. David uses the beautiful parallelism of Hebrew poetry to convey these truths. David also realizes such wonderful revelation and communication from God necessitates a response. So, his request is for the cleansing of his sin so that what he does, says, and thinks will be pleasing to God (vv. 12–14).

## Digging In

In verses 1–6, David looks to the heavenly host in wonder at how they declare the glory and knowledge of God. First, he focuses on the heavens in general, and then he narrows his focus to the sun. Verse 1 uses synonymous parallelism with three words in the second line matching the three words in the first. The pairs are "heavens" and the "expanse," "declare" and "proclaims," and "the glory of God" and "the work of his hands." The "heavens" and "expanse" both refer to the skies and everything in space beyond. The words *declare* and *proclaims* are participles in Hebrew, meaning the heavens and expanse are continually declaring and proclaiming as verse 2 also asserts. By recognizing the first two pairs are synonyms, it reveals that the third pair are synonyms too. So, David is saying that "the work of his hands" witnesses to "the glory of God." "The work of his hands" means all of the skies and space above are God's creation. The word *glory* means heaviness or weightiness. So, David is saying God's creation of the heavens gives weight to who God is. He is transcendent, above the highest reaches of space. He is of ultimate importance; there is none like him. Without words, the heavens pour out this knowledge of God's omnipotence, his wisdom, and grandeur for everyone to see.

Most notable of all the heavenly hosts is the sun. David uses similes to describe its splendor. The heavens stand over it like a tent. Like a bridegroom and an athlete, the sun is brilliant and strong. It provides warmth and sustenance for the entire Earth (vv. 4b–6). The sun is central to life on the earth. It affects the oceans and the weather, providing energy for the plants to grow which in turn provide oxygen and nourishment for life on Earth. Without the sun, we could not survive. The sun not only reveals the power and beauty of God but also the wisdom and goodness of God to provide for all of physical life on Earth.

Likewise, God has provided for our spiritual lives by the revelation of his Word. Once again, employing the beauty of Hebrew parallelism, David expounds the blessing and centrality of God's Word to all of life. Without God's Word, we could not survive. Creation reveals the glory of God; God's Word reveals the way to God. How? The tender "instruction" of God restores vitality to the spiritually infirmed and life to the spiritually dead (v. 7a). The "testimony of the LORD," all of what God has told his people, is trustworthy, giving wisdom to the one who needs it (v. 7b). It reveals the danger of being out of God's will even when one is unaware of it. God's "precepts" are entirely right, not a burden but a source of joy for those who obey them. The "command of the LORD," the entirety of his revealed Word, cleanses one's eyes, giving one a clear perspective of life. It lights up the eyes revealing the inner joy God's Word brings (v. 8). The "fear of the LORD" gives instruction on what it means to reverence Yahweh in awe. It is pure and eternal. The "ordinances," God's judgments on matters, inform us of what is appropriate conduct. Therefore, they are "reliable and altogether righteous" (v. 9). Nothing compares to the value of God's Word. The wise will desire it more than anything else in life. True satisfaction and delight comes from the sweetness of knowing God's Word and faithfully living in accordance to it. Moreover, God's Word both warns one of dangers that would ruin one's life and rewards one for listening to it and obeying (vv. 10–11).

David displays the proper response to having witnessed God's revelation of himself in both his creation and his Word—a prayer for cleansing and purity. David's concern is not only for the willful sin he is aware of in his life, but he also is troubled by the unknown sin in his life. Our sin nature has such a grip on us that we often sin unintentionally and unawarely. The Law of Moses recognizes this truth and provides the Sin Offering as a means of atonement for unintentional sins and the sins one unawarely commits (Lev. 4:1–5:13). David's desire is to live completely devoted to Yahweh in every way. He wants the Lord, not his sin, to rule his life. He realizes he cannot keep from ever sinning, but he is asking the Lord to help him be godly (v. 13). His prayer is for everything he says and thinks to be acceptable to Yahweh. He is offering himself as a living sacrifice to his rock, his strength and foundation in life, his Redeemer, his protector, provider, and savior (v. 14).

## Living It Out

Psalm 19 demonstrates that God wants us to know him. He has demonstrated this in creation, by his Word, and ultimately through his Son, the Lord Jesus Christ (Heb. 1:1–4). Like David, we should praise God as we witness the splendor of God's handiwork. However, as wonderful as God's creation is, even more magnificent is his written Word. For it is God's Word that shows us how to know our Creator. We need to be in God's Word because it is what revives us, guides us, and sustains us. It is also what leads us to Jesus Christ, the living Word who became flesh according to the apostle John (John 1:14). It is because of the person and work of Jesus Christ that we can be cleansed of our sin and made right with God. <u>Therefore, let us seek to know our Lord who</u> graciously invites us to know him.

*and praise him for what He has made known rather than giving into frustration over what we cannot grasp*

# The King's Victory

*Psalms 20–21*

## The Big Picture

Psalms 20 and 21 are royal psalms, psalms in which the king is a prominent figure. Psalm 20 is a prayer uttered by his people, his army, and the king himself asking God to give the king the victory as he prepares to go to battle. It is an antiphony, which is the responsive alternation between two parties, in this case, between either the people or his army and the king. Psalm 21 is a song of thanksgiving and praise after battle because the victory has been won and the Lord has answered their prayer. Apparently, it was common for the king along with his army and the people to gather together for prayer in preparation for battle (see 2 Chron. 20). The particular occasion for these prayers is unknown, but David led his army into battle many times, so these psalms likely were part of the tradition of pre-battle regimen. No doubt, they also serve as words of encouragement to those facing the challenges and spiritual battles that often accompany serving the Lord.

## Digging In

[Psalm 20 begins with the people's prayer of intercession for the king in verses 1–5b. These requests are a demonstration of their dependence and trust in God.] Their first request is for the Lord to protect the king from literally getting into a "tight spot" by "setting him on high" (making him unreachable) in the heat of battle. The expression, "the name of Jacob's God," means Yahweh is the God who promised their forefathers to bless them and protect them from their enemies. His name carries with it the promise of all the attributes of God as Yahweh committed himself in a loving, faithful covenant relationship to Jacob and his descendants (v. 1).

They begin the prayer after the king has made sacrifices to the Lord, beseeching Yahweh's help in leading the army to victory. These offerings would have been made at the sanctuary on Mount Zion in Jerusalem. It was the location of the tabernacle in David's day and the location of the temple Solomon built for later kings. Therefore, their second request is for the Lord to respond favorably to the king's supplications and offerings that demonstrated his submission to God, his acceptance by God, and his commitment to God (vv. 2–3). The third request is that the Lord gives the king victory and that his battle plans are in line with God's will. It is the meshing of human effort with God's providence. [David prepared as best he could and should, but in the end he realized everything was in God's hands (v. 4).]

In the beginning of verse 5, the people exclaim their confidence in God to hear their requests and grant victory to David. Usually, people don't express their joy until what they have requested has happened. But here, the people rejoice ahead of time because they believe in their God to give them the victory. They anticipate lifting their banners in celebration of what their God has done when their king and his army returns the victors. At the end of verse 5, the people summarize what they have said saying to the king, "May the LORD fulfill all your requests."

[It is at this point the king responds, declaring his confidence in the Lord. He knows it is Yahweh who will save his anointed, giving him victory.] The Almighty will answer these requests with a colossal display of his power from his throne in heaven (v. 6). Everyone then sings together in verses 7–8. These verses contrast those who trust in their own resources with those who trust in God. The enemy takes pride in their manufactured implements of war along with their war horses. The people of God trust in the name of the Lord their God. Proverbs 18:10 states, "The name of the LORD is a strong tower; the righteous run to it and are protected." [As stated previously, to trust in the name of the Lord is to trust in him, his character, his promises and attributes. How can chariots and horses compare to or stand up to the name of the Lord?] Therefore, it is no surprise that those who trust in chariots and horses will fall while those whose confidence is in the name of the Lord will "rise and stand firm." Psalm 20 ends with the people making one final request, asking the Lord to answer their prayer (v. 9).

Psalm 21 is the answer to their prayer. The psalm begins and ends praising the Lord for his strength. (vv. 1, 13). The body of Psalm 21 is divided into two sections. Verses 2–7 list the blessings the Lord has bestowed upon the king, and verses 8–12 list the curses God has in store for his enemies. So, how has the Lord blessed David? ① God answered his prayer by giving him victory in battle. ② God went with him in battle and richly blessed him by honoring him with the crown of the defeated. ③ The Lord saved his life and will ultimately save him for eternity. ④ God gave David victory and glory in battle to put on full display to both his enemies and the people that, in truth, the victory and glory belongs to the Lord. ⑤ David is and eternally will be blessed with the joy of God's presence. And ⑥ because of Yahweh's faithful, covenant love, the king confidently relies on him.

According to verses 8–12, what will the Lord do to his enemies? He will destroy them. He will seize them and consume them with fire. There is nothing more devastating than fire because it almost totally consumes whatever it touches. Little but ash remains. So, the language of fire and the eradication of the offspring of his enemies is a potent way of saying they will be totally defeated and destroyed, no longer a threat to the people of God. Though the enemies' intent is to harm the people of God, they will fail. Again, David concludes the same way he introduced his song, praising the Lord for his strength (v. 13).

## Living It Out

Together, Psalms 20 and 21 provide a picture of how believers should approach challenges and spiritual battles. We need to offer ourselves to God as living sacrifices in submission and commitment, recognizing that, by the sacrifice of the Lord Jesus Christ, we are acceptable to God. Then, we should make our requests to God with confident expectation and joy because we belong to him and he is faithful to his own. We must dedicate our plans to him, trust in the strength of his name and pray that his will be done. Our desire needs to be his glory. In addition, when we have witnessed his deliverance, we must acknowledge what God has done and praise his name as a testimony to all who hear that the Lord alone is worthy of our praise. For he has done great things, and more is yet to come.

# From Feeling Abandoned to Exclamations of Praise

*Psalm 22*

## The Big Picture

Psalm 22 is a psalm of personal lament, a cry to God in the midst of personal difficulty. It is difficult to know exactly when David experienced what he describes in Psalm 22. There are plenty of times he was besieged by his enemies. Some Bible scholars believe he could not have really experienced what the psalm describes because of the extreme expressions of grief and suffering described in it. It appears to be metaphorical to them or exaggeration and hyperbolic. But how can anyone else but the Lord know what David experienced, much less what he felt? Psalm 22 begins with David's sense of God's abandonment but concludes with his exclamations of praise as he experiences the Lord's salvation.

Psalm 22 also typologically serves as a foreshadowing of Jesus' suffering on the cross. In fact, Jesus at least quoted verse 1 and it is possible that he actually recited the entire prayer (Matt. 27:46). Several

parts of Psalm 22 describe what Jesus experienced when he was cru-
cified: 1) his sensing God's abandonment (22:1; Matt. 27:46); 2) his
being scorned and mocked (22:7–8; Matt. 27:41–42; Luke 23:35–36);
3) his suffering (22:14–15a); 4) his thirst (22:14–15; John 19:28); 5) the
piercing of his hands and feet (22:16; Luke 24:39–40; John 20:20); and
6) his garments being divided by the casting of lots (22:18; Matt. 27:35;
Mark 15:24; Luke 23:34; John 19:23–24). However, Psalm 22:27 also
anticipates the triumph of Christ when "all the families of the nations
will bow down before you." The apostle Paul wrote "every knee will
bow—in heaven and on the earth—and under the earth and every
tongue will confess that Jesus Christ is Lord, to the glory of God the
Father" (Phil. 2:10–11).

## Digging In

Psalm 22 may be separated into three sections. Verses 1–11
describe David's sense of abandonment by God, verses 12–21a describe
David's abuse by his enemies, and verses 21b–31 declare David's adora-
tion of the Lord because God has answered his prayer and rescued him.

In the first section, David expresses his sense of God's abandonment with three questions: 1) "Why have you abandoned me?" 2) "Why
won't you save me?" And 3) "Why won't you hear my groaning?" The
first question expresses David's confusion over how the God who hears
the prayers of his people has apparently turned a deaf ear to one of his
servants. His frustration and distress are expounded by the following
two questions accompanied by his restless cries day and night (v. 2).
One must recognize that while David felt like God had abandoned
him, God did not abandon David as we will see in verse 24. However,
when Jesus cried out these words to his Father, God actually did abandon him on the cross. It is difficult to comprehend how Jesus bore our
sin and in so doing experienced the wrath of God, our due penalty for
our sin. Being forsaken by God is the predicament of the damned, and
at Cavalry, Jesus took upon himself the full weight of our damnation.
The Father abandoned the Son so that we could receive the Father's
promise: "I will never leave you or abandon you" (Heb. 13:5).

In verses 3–5, David remembers how God has been faithful in the past to answer the prayers of his forefathers when they needed to be rescued from trouble. [They trusted in the Lord, and they were not disgraced by what would have appeared to have been misplaced trust in Yahweh if he had not responded to their cries.] The point is David also trusts in the Lord. However, David is being disgraced by those who sneer at him and mock him all because of his faith in the Lord. In their eyes, he is a worthless "worm" and an object of ridicule. Their mockery was not only against David but also against the Lord, insolently asserting Yahweh cannot save you from us (vv. 6–8). Then, David ends this section reminding God how he has trusted and served the Lord for his entire life. Hence, he again pleads for God's help (vv. 9–11).

In verses 12–21a, with poetic imagery David describes his enemies' hostile actions and their effects on him. They are like the massive bulls of Bashan, the largest and strongest bulls in the region, representing the enormity of the threat to David. They are like lions ready to maul and consume him. They are like a pack of dogs ready to scavenge what is left of his carcass. As a result, David is weak, in anguish, gaunt (probably meaning he is so upset he is unable to eat), losing all hope. He is physically, emotionally, and spiritually spent. Saying his garments were divided among them is David's way of saying, "I'm a dead man," since the deceased no longer need clothing. After describing the enemies and their effects on him, David again cries to the Lord to deliver him from the sword, the dogs, the lion, and the wild oxen, all expressions describing his enemies who seek his death. Because the Lord is David's source of strength, David emphatically pleads with Yahweh, "don't be far away" (v. 19).

At the end of verse 21, there is a dramatic change. Here David exclaims, "You answered me!" After this declaration, the psalm contains no more begging for help. Somehow, David discovers the Lord has either answered his cry or is about to, and the remaining section of the psalm is one of declarative praise. It is the heartfelt response of one who was in a life-threatening situation and has been rescued out of it. He wants everyone to hear how the Lord saved him. What's more, he wants other believers to join him in praising the Lord. Why? Because Yahweh heard his prayer and delivered him from his predicament

(vv. 21a–24). As David offers a sacrifice of thanksgiving to the Lord in his sanctuary, the people of God will join David in the celebration.

David concludes the psalm with his anticipation of God's rule over all the nations as multitudes from every people group on the earth come to faith and worship the Lord. Future generations will come to saving faith in the Lord because they have heard of his righteousness, the God who never abandons his people. These future generations will pass the good news of God's salvation to their children, and they, too, will serve the Lord. What will their message be? It will be a proclamation of what the Lord has done.

## Living It Out

We should look at Psalm 22 from two perspectives: what we learn from David's experience and what we learn from the Lord Jesus Christ on the cross. David shows us that even when it appears God is not listening to our prayers, he really is. So, we need to pray more, not less, in those situations. Also, we need to remember God's faithfulness in the past, when we have difficulty seeing it in the present. On the cross, Jesus' suffering shows us what God was willing to do to demonstrate his love for us and save us from our sin. Moreover, because God abandoned Jesus on the cross, we can be assured God will never abandon us.

# My Shepherd

*Psalm 23*

## The Big Picture

There likely is no other passage more recognized or beloved from the Scriptures than Psalm 23. In one sense, such familiarity is a good thing, but in another sense, it might prohibit one from taking the time to carefully examine the gold mine that is Psalm 23. Its original context or setting is unknown, but in it, David the shepherd recognizes the Lord as his Shepherd and expresses his trust and confidence in him. Knowing only God is willing and able to provide for his every need, David expresses his total dependence on him. Psalm 23 should give comfort to every believer as it emphasizes the Lord's constant tender care for his people both now and for eternity. In only fifty-five words in the original Hebrew language, David succinctly conveys the abundant grace our Lord bestows upon us as our Shepherd.

## Digging In

Psalm 23 begins with David, the shepherd who became a king, recognizing he is but a sheep who needs a shepherd. It demonstrates the complete humility and dependence on God he must have had to have sincerely written these words. And his use of the name, "LORD" or Yahweh, God's personal, covenant name to Israel touches on the idea that the Lord is unchanging and unchangeable. He is self-sustaining and self-existent. He Was, and Is, and Will Be from everlasting to everlasting. Hence, the expression "the LORD is my shepherd" is both corporate and personal at the same time—corporate as it relates to God's covenantal name to all of Israel and, at the same time, personal in that David uses the word *my* as opposed to "our."

Shepherding is one of the earliest occupations in ancient history. Their job included feeding and watering the flock; protecting the flock from danger; caring for the hygiene of each sheep; and at times disciplining a sheep. The word *shepherd* in the Old Testament not only pertains to shepherds in the fields with the flocks but it is also a synonym for king. Many times the Old Testament writers call kings shepherds. As shepherds, the kings of Israel were responsible for all the needs of their people, their flock per se. So whether they are in the fields or on a throne, shepherds are to provide for every need of their sheep. David declares that because the Lord is his shepherd, he has everything he needs. There is no deficiency in the Lord's provision (v. 1).

The "green pastures" speak of Yahweh's generous provision, and the "quiet waters" speak of a place of peaceful rest. Sheep are easily frightened, and so are a lot of people, but the believer whose confidence is in the Lord may trust in the faithful provision and the sacred security that comes from following him. Thus, it is a picture of the Lord's guiding presence with his sheep (v. 2).

In verse 3, the word *renews* means to bring back to its place of departure, to restore. One could read it literally as "he restores life to life." The Bible reveals that God uses his Word to restore us as we previously saw in Psalm 19:7–8. He has also given us the people of God to restore us (1 Thess. 5:11). Ultimately, though, God has given us his Son, the Lord Jesus Christ, to "have life and have it in abundance" (John 10:10).

The second half of verse 3 declares that Yahweh also leads his sheep along worn paths of righteousness for the sake of his name. Following the Lord means developing a lifestyle that will become a lifetime of habits that, when taken altogether, culminate in a righteous life, well-lived for the glory of God, "for his name's sake." God's faithfulness to lead his people along "right paths" is a reflection of his reputation. Samuel the prophet said, "The LORD will not abandon his people, because of his great name" (1 Sam. 12:22).

Sometimes shepherds needed to lead their flock through the narrow, serpentine wadis or canyons in Israel beset with dark shadows to get their flocks to better pastures on the other side. David is talking about difficult times in life, death, or both. Whichever, David's shepherd will always be with him, and knowledge of this truth wipes away all his fears. David emphatically states that the shepherd's rod used to correct, protect, and count the sheep, and his staff, which is used to guide the flock and rescue those sheep that get themselves into tight spots, both comfort him (v. 4).

Verse 5 changes from Yahweh the shepherd to Yahweh the host. David says the Lord prepares a meal for him, and since the Lord is his host, David is under Yahweh's protection and care. In Israel's culture, the host assumed full responsibility for the safety of their guests. Consequently, David's enemy is no threat to him. The scene may anticipate a victory celebration like those practiced in the ancient Near East, where the captive enemies are taunted with being forced to watch the banquet. The second part of verse 5 refers to the ancient custom of a caring host rubbing a guest's head with perfumed oil as a refreshing gesture of hospitality (Luke 7:46). "My cup overflows" proclaims Yahweh's abundant blessing on David's life.

David says, "only goodness and faithful love will pursue me all the days of my life." "Goodness" speaks of that which promotes, protects, produces and enhances life. "Faithful love" is the word *hesed* in Hebrew and it is Yahweh's covenant love, loyalty, zealous commitment, faithfulness, graciousness, mercy, and favor all wrapped up in one word. No word alone in English can capture its meaning. Such "goodness" and "faithful love" will determinedly and successfully chase David all the days of his life. And in response to such goodness and faithful love, David's desire is to spend the rest of his days worshiping the Lord (v. 6).

## Living It Out

Like David, as believers we have every reason to place our complete trust and confidence in the Lord, who is our shepherd—yours and mine. Our relationship to him is both corporate and personal. We must love the flock as he does. Whenever we have a need, we must remember the Lord is all we need for he will not neglect his own. His reputation is at stake. We must remember that in the most difficult times, he is with us to tenderly protect and provide for us. Even in death, the Lord Jesus, the Good Shepherd, has laid down his life for his sheep so that we will securely spend eternity with him (John 10:11–18).

# The King of Glory

*Psalm 24*

## The Big Picture

[Psalm 24 is most likely a song depicting David and his victorious army after battle, returning to the sanctuary in Jerusalem to worship the Lord and return the ark of the covenant.]There are three sections to Psalm 24. Verses 1–2 declare Yahweh's authority over all creation because the Lord is the Creator. Verses 3–6 attest to the Lord's particularity when it comes to who may approach and enter his sanctuary to worship him. Not just anyone is accepted. Then, verses 7–10 focus on Yahweh, the King of glory, who triumphantly leads his armies back to Jerusalem after a glorious victory over their enemies and then enters his holy sanctuary.

## Digging In

Psalm 24 begins with a declaration of God's authority over all the earth and everything in it because he is the one who created all of it (vv. 1–2). It is for this reason, when reading Genesis 1:1, one should recognize it is more than just an answer to the questions, "How did the universe begin, and how did we get here?" It is that, but it is more than that. The statement, "In the beginning God created the heavens and the earth," establishes God's power and authority over creation since he is the Creator. This concept is essential to understanding God's right to choose Israel as his "own possession out of all the peoples," and it was at the heart of the prophet Amos's message of judgment to Israel (Exod. 19:5; Amos 4:13; 5:8–9).

In Psalm 24:1, David is saying that since the Lord is the Creator, not only does it all belong to him, but he can do with it whatever he pleases. So David begins this song about the triumphant King of glory, he proclaims that their God, the God who gave them victory over their enemies, is sovereign over all his creation, over everything and everyone. This kind of thinking was foreign to other nations. In the ancient Near East, each nation believed the gods were sovereign over their own nations. So to them, Yahweh's authority went only as far as the boundaries of Israel just as Ashur's power was limited to Assyria's boundaries. Gods were thought of as being regional with the understanding that conquering the land of other gods then diminished their rule as the conquering god extended his regional dominion. The concept of one God who is the creator of all things and sovereign over everything, however, was quite unusual.

Verse 2 observes that the Lord laid the earth's foundations on the seas and established it on the rivers. It is an ancient and poetic way of recognizing how the dry ground separates the seas and how springs and rivers flow underground. Also, given the context of Psalm 24 being a song of triumph over Israel's enemies, this verse could be a way of taunting Israel's enemies by alluding to Yahweh's victory over their gods of chaos represented by the seas. In the minds of the pagans, Israel's victory over their enemies was a tangible way of witnessing Yahweh's victory over the gods of their enemies in the spiritual realm. In other words, it could have been a way of mocking their enemies using their enemies' language and expression.

Reminiscent of Psalm 15, Psalm 24:3–6 describes who is permitted to approach God's sanctuary and whose worship is acceptable to him. The Lord is particular about who can worship him. The sanctuary is "his holy place." It is the place devoted to Yahweh, therefore the people who worship him must be holy to the Lord, devoted to him. This is what is meant by "the one who has clean hands and a pure heart." It is the person who obeys God's Word with a faithful heart—outward commitment that springs from an inner devotion to the Lord. It is a person of integrity. Such individuals will receive God's favor and vindication of their faith in God by his blessing. In the context of the psalm, their victory over their enemies is vindication that their faith in Yahweh was well placed. Such will be the case for those who have a sincere desire to live for God. These people are the true Israel (see Rom. 9:6). Being physically born a child of Jacob (whose name was changed to Israel by God) does not automatically qualify one to be acceptable to God.

The final section, Psalm 24:7–10, announces and exalts the Lord as his triumphal procession approaches the sanctuary. As mentioned above, this would have involved the ark of the covenant. The ark of the covenant was designed for mobility with a rectangular shape about four feet long and two and a half feet wide and deep. It represented the presence of God and had aspects of it that were similar to designs on the thrones in the ancient Near East. Only Levitical priests were allowed to carry it suspended on two long poles. The ark played an important role as Israel went to war because it was at the front of the troops indicating that the Lord was going before them into battle. So, verses 7–10 are a depiction of Yahweh, the King of glory, leading his troops triumphantly back home. Poetically speaking, the heads of the doors should lift up in joyous celebration from their bowed prayers of concern for the men in battle. Yahweh is the King of glory; Yahweh is a mighty Warrior. It is the Lord who fights mightily for his people and leads them to triumphant victory.

## Living It Out

Psalm 24 highlights how essential it is for believers to recognize the Lord's authority over all creation. Everything belongs to him, and he has the right to do what pleases him. Consequently, he has the right to dictate what worship is acceptable and unacceptable. We come to him his way or we do not come to him at all. And what is his way? If we want the Lord to accept our worship, we first must recognize that we come to him through the righteousness of our Lord Jesus Christ. However, if we are living in wanton disobedience to Christ, God will not accept our attempts to worship him. Jesus teaches that we need to make things right with those we have offended before we worship the Lord (Matt. 5:23), and that includes offending the Lord himself. [Psalm 24 reminds us there is great blessing in loving the Lord and seeking to live for him.] We can trust that he is our mighty Warrior who fights on our behalf as he has defeated sin, death, and the works of the devil. Some day we will march in triumphal victory as he leads us to his eternal throne.

# Deliverance, Guidance, and Forgiveness

*Psalm 25*

## The Big Picture

Psalm 25 is an individual lament expressing the need for God's deliverance, guidance, and forgiveness. The structure of this psalm is unusual and difficult as it repeats its themes throughout. In Hebrew, with minor emendations, it is an acrostic poem with each of the lines beginning with a letter of the Hebrew alphabet except the last verse, which serves as a kind of "amen" or benediction to the psalm. It is also difficult to pinpoint when David wrote this psalm. He spent a great amount of time living with the threat of enemies. Furthermore, with so much emphasis on the need for forgiveness it could be in response to David's sin of adultery, but the psalm also speaks of the "sins of [his] youth" (v. 7). The general nature of his self-examination suggests the psalm is more about David's personal sensitivity to his failures in general and his desire for forgiveness and guidance so that he can faithfully live for God.

## Digging In

The psalm begins with an emphatic plea for deliverance. Literally, David cries out, "To you LORD, my life I lift up!" He lifts his life to Yahweh because Yahweh is the only one he can trust with his life. Yahweh is David's covenantal God who keeps his divine promises to his people. So, David turns to God in submission and anticipation of God's deliverance. In verses 2–3, David uses the word *disgraced* three times, demonstrating the gravity of his concern. The disgrace would be David's being destroyed by his enemies. He prays what he knows to be true. When one prays what God has revealed about himself to be true, one can be assured that God will hear and answer the prayer. David knows the Lord will not allow those who put their trust in him to be put to shame. Instead, their faith in God will be vindicated. It will be those who treacherously seek to put David to shame by gloating over him who will be put to shame. The would-be destroyers will become the destroyed.

In verses 4–7, David submissively asks for guidance and forgiveness because he recognizes his own inadequacy. David's desire is to do God's will, so he prays for Yahweh to make known his ways, teach him his paths, and to guide him in his truth—"show me, teach me, guide me, teach me." Why does he seek to line up his life with the will of God? It is because Yahweh is the God of his salvation. David's desire is the natural response of one who has experienced the Lord's salvation. Therefore he is continuing to trust in God's salvation for the present and eternity. He trusts the Lord for the strength and wisdom to walk in his ways. For this reason, David waits in confident anticipation for the Lord to answer his prayer (v. 5c).

Next, in verses 6–7, David prays for God's forgiveness. He prays to God, "remember" and "do not remember." It is not speaking of cognitive memory per se, but David is asking God to act upon his mercy and not in accordance to David's sins. David knows he is unable and unfit to atone for his own sins. He is depending on the Lord's mercy and compassion. David is also depending on Yahweh's faithful love, his *hesed*, in Hebrew. Again, David looks to the Lord's covenant love, loyalty, zealous commitment, faithfulness, kindness, graciousness, mercy, and favor. No one word in English can adequately translate its meaning. David is asking God to act now on David's behalf as God has always acted on behalf of his people. Consequently, David confidently asks the Lord to forget the sins of his youth and his acts of rebellion. He is asking God to let the past stay in the past. Why should the Lord do this? It is because of the Lord's goodness. David knew the same truth that Jesus told the rich young ruler: "No one is good except God alone" (Luke 18:19). This truth must have comforted David as he prayed for God's forgiveness.

[When David thinks about God's goodness, he cannot help but praise the Lord.] It is because God is good and upright that he graciously leads humble sinners in his way. It is only his kind revelation of himself to sinners that makes it possible for them to know and follow his way. Everything God does demonstrates his faithful love *(hesed)* and truth to those who live in faithful obedience to him.

Verse 11 contains the center and climax of David's prayer. [The main reason God should forgive David is for the sake of Yahweh's name or reputation.] David reveals the heart of one who truly desires to live for God because his primary concern is God's glory and reputation and not his own. David's identity is wrapped up in God's identity. The actions of the people of God reflect on Yahweh's reputation, and God's actions toward his people reflect on his reputation. If God's purpose is to use his people as a witness to the nations of who he is, then what would his refusal to forgive his repentant followers say about him?

Therefore, verses 12–14 reveal David's confident anticipation of God's blessing. The person who fears the Lord is the person who acknowledges the awesome majesty of God and obeys him joyfully and submissively. It is this person who can expect the Lord to guide him, to give him a good life, and to bless his descendants. God will give intimate counsel to them as a loving, wise father or mother would to a son or daughter.

In verses 15–21, David returns to where he began in the psalm asking God for deliverance. He begins and ends with a word of confidence, declaring the Lord "will pull my feet out of the net" (v. 15) and concluding with "I wait for you" (v. 21). David describes himself as alone, afflicted, distressed, suffering, and troubled. David reveals the cause of his affliction and trouble is because of sins, so he asks for his compassionate God's forgiveness (v. 18).[And once again David asks God to not let him be disgraced or put to shame because David has taken refuge in the Lord.]Here David connects his deliverance with both his and God's entwined reputations. David knows integrity and what is right will protect those who trust in the Lord's salvation (v. 21). In verse 22, David remembers that he is not alone in his need for God. Truly godly believers will remember to pray for the people of God.

## Living It Out

Psalm 25 should remind believers of a number of important truths. First, if we need to be saved, God is a saving God. Cast your cares upon him because he cares for you (1 Pet. 5:7). Second, when we need guidance, we need to look to the Lord and his Word. He will lead us and teach us in his ways. Third, if we need forgiveness, God is a compassionate God who is ready and willing to forgive a repentant soul. He receives sinners, we receive Christ, and then he receives our prayers. Therefore, we must never forget that God is good. We can trust him even when we do not always perceive or understand him or his ways.

## Day Nineteen

# A Prayer for Vindication

*Psalm 26*

## The Big Picture

We saw in Psalm 25 David's desire for Yahweh to teach him his ways and guide him. [In Psalm 26, David makes the case that he has received Yahweh's instruction and has devoted himself to receive his guidance by living according to Yahweh's truth (v. 3).] David demonstrates his commitment by expressing his love for worshiping the Lord in his sanctuary. Therefore, because of his faithfulness to Yahweh, David's prayer is for Yahweh's vindication, to justify David's devotion to Yahweh, to uphold and defend David against his opposition and to save him from the ill fate of sinners. The structure of Psalm 25 begins with David's plea for vindication (vv. 1–2). This is followed by David's description of his faithfulness to Yahweh (vv. 3–8). And then, the last section is David's request for the Lord to save him from the destined destruction of sinners (vv. 9–11). Verse 12 concludes the psalm with a vow to praise the Lord in the sanctuary.

## Digging In

As we have seen in previous psalms, David has expressed a tremendous concern for the Lord to vindicate him (e.g., Pss. 7:8; 9:4; 17:2; 43:1). The word _vindicate_ has several nuances of meaning. It can mean to clear one's name of false accusations. It can mean to justify or show that one has done the right thing in a matter. It can even mean to plead the case of someone, to maintain and defend one against opposition. David knew what it was like to suffer false accusations from his enemies like those who were in Saul's court saying David was plotting to kill the king (1 Sam. 24:9; see also Pss. 10; 12:1–4). Many times, David had appealed to the Lord to show that David did what was right before God. He made this appeal to the Lord to judge between him and Saul and show that he was right and that it was Saul who did wrongly (1 Sam. 24:12). David also prayed that the Lord would plead his case and deliver him from Saul (1 Sam. 24:15). In addition, on numerous occasions, David prayed God would demonstrate David was right to put his trust in the Lord (e.g., Ps. 16:1).

David begins Psalm 26 praying "Vindicate me, LORD." The occasion for this plea is unclear, but David attests that the reason the Lord should vindicate him is because of David's unwavering commitment to live for Yahweh. David believes that if the Lord would examine his life, the Lord would see that David is a man of integrity, the kind of man God vindicates. David's saying he has lived with integrity means he has lived in total devotion to the Lord; and understanding it is impossible to please God without faith, David affirms that his faith in the Lord has been unwavering. "Without wavering" not only speaks of David's trust but more importantly of Yahweh's faithfulness to uphold him and keep him from wavering (v. 1). Then, he invites the Lord to test him so that he can show what he is saying is true. The Lord already knows David's heart, but David wants the opportunity to demonstrate his loyalty and also to be made aware of any failures so that they can be corrected. By asking the Lord to examine his heart and mind, David is expressing his desire for total dedication to God (v. 2).

Next, David affirms his devotion to the Lord by providing evidence of it in his life. This evidence is displayed both by what he does and does not do. The all-consuming focus of David's life is Yahweh's faithful, covenantal love, his *hesed*, which speaks of all the provisions and promises of God's gracious covenant with his people. Moreover, he lives his life by Yahweh's "truth," the Lord's unfailing reliability and trustworthiness. David's focus is clear and his foundation is true (v. 3).

On the other hand, David insists that he has completely disassociated himself from wickedness and those who perpetrate wrongdoing. The worthless seek after things that don't matter in life and lead to a dead end. The hypocrites are deceptive and cloaked in false piety. The assembly of evildoers and the wicked are those who are within the community of the people of God who really are not devoted to God. They have chosen to reject Yahweh and go their own way. David has chosen the way of the blessed man of Psalm 1:1 (vv. 4–5).

Therefore, he can be found with the assembly of the people of God in the Lord's sanctuary joyfully worshiping him. The idea of washing his hands may refer to ritualistic cleansing, but it is more likely that he is affirming his innocence before God, indicating it is acceptable for him to approach the Lord to worship at his altar (v. 6). It echoes Psalm 24:3–4a, "Who may ascend the mountain of the LORD? Who may stand in his holy place? The one who has clean hands and a pure heart." His purpose for approaching the altar is to raise his "voice in thanksgiving" and exclaim God's "wondrous works." David wants all to hear about how wonderful the Lord is. Additionally, the Lord's house is David's refuge, and he cannot help proclaiming his love for the house of God where God manifests his presence and his awesome glory before his people (v. 7).

David's plea for vindication concludes with asking the Lord to withhold from him the judgment God has in store for the wicked. This would be a sign that David has been right to trust in God and that David is truly a man of God. Unlike David, these sinners are men who have shed innocent blood. They scheme to cause harm to the innocent and are motivated by selfish gain. In his just wrath, God will destroy these sinners (vv. 9–10). However, David is not with them now and will not be among them on the day of the Lord's final judgment. David knows in whom he has believed and lives for him. Consequently, David rests in the Lord's gracious salvation (v. 11). Furthermore, because of this, he stands on a firm foundation of faith in the God whose ways are faithful. And as he does this, David will bless the Lord with his worship to extol him before the people of God.

## Living It Out

In Psalm 26, David may appear to be self-righteous and braggadocios about it, but that is far from the truth. David expresses a desire to live a life completely devoted to God. It is the desire of every faithful believer. David provides an example of how we should praise the Lord for guiding us and giving us his Word as a firm foundation for life. Like David, we too must shun sin and enjoy the company of believers. We must recognize that the Lord himself is our greatest treasure and worshiping him is our greatest joy. Likewise, we should be ardent in voicing our thanksgiving to God, praising him for who he is and seeking to be a blessing to him.

# My Stronghold and My Strength

*Psalms 27–28*

## The Big Picture

It is difficult to pinpoint the occasion David wrote these psalms, but Psalms 27 and 28 express confidence in the Lord's salvation and justice as David's enemies harass him. Psalms 27 and 28 have similarities with Psalm 26. Like Psalm 26, Psalms 27 and 28 refer to worship in the Lord's sanctuary, express dependence on the Lord and trust in his deliverance. Additionally, Psalms 27 and 28 share a literary connection. The structure of Psalm 28 is the opposite of Psalm 27. Psalm 27 begins with David confidently praising God followed by David's lament; Psalm 28 begins with David's lament followed by praise. Together they form a chiasm.

## Digging In

Psalm 27 commences with a declaration of David's confidence in Yahweh as he asserts that the Lord is his "light," "salvation," and "stronghold of life." [As David's light, the Lord vanquishes the powers of darkness, as David's salvation the Lord is his deliverer, and as David's stronghold, the Lord is his guardian] How can David be afraid of his enemies when the Lord is his protector? The Lord who has rescued David from enemies with violent intent in the past will surely defend him now and in the future. No matter how colossal the enemy threat may be, David will be confident because of his God.

Therefore, David expresses but one longing: "to dwell in the house of the LORD all the days of my life" (v. 4). David articulates that this has been his desire and it will continue to be his desire. Why? [David yearns to gaze "on the beauty of the LORD," to witness the wonders he performs for his people] Also, David wishes to seek the Lord's instruction and guidance. Moreover, David recognizes no place is more secure for him. Being in the Lord's sanctuary positively affects David's perspective. There he knows the Lord will conceal him from his enemies and set him on a high rock where his enemies cannot reach him (v. 5). [In his secure position, David anticipates looking down at his distant enemies and vows to worship the Lord with loud songs of joy (v. 6).]

In verses 7–12, David's tone changes as he cries out to God to hear his voice and deliver him from his adversaries. [The emphasis is on the Lord's "face." David's innermost longing is to seek God's face.] To seek the Lord's face is to seek his presence and the grace of God that comes with his presence. As David indicated, being in God's presence gives David a right perspective on his situation. And while it is true that God is always present with his people, believers sometimes have difficulty recognizing God's presence because of their fallen nature or difficult circumstances. David realized God has been his "helper" and that he would be doomed without God. Nonetheless, in his anguish, David knows the Lord cares for him. Therefore, because of his adversaries David asks the Lord to show him what is right and lead him to do what is right. David also asks the Lord to deliver him from his enemies who lie about him and seek to harm him.

David concludes Psalm 27 with a declaration of his confidence in the Lord. He is convinced of God's goodness and that he will experience his salvation. Hence, with strength and courage, he is determined to wait on the Lord who will not disappoint him (vv. 13–14).

Psalm 28 begins with David's lament, connecting it to Psalm 27 where we see he started his lament in verse 7 saying, "Lord, hear my voice when I call," and in Psalm 28:1 he emphatically cries out, "Lord, I call to you." Both verses express David's dependence on God. David continues to express his dependence on God by calling him "my rock." God is his rock who gives him strength and sustenance just as he did the children of Israel from the rock in the wilderness (Num. 20:11). The apostle Paul indicates Jesus Christ was the spiritual rock with his people in the Old Testament.

God's silence troubles David because it could be a sign of God's discipline and indicate God may not intervene for David. The Lord's silence is unbearable, and David feels like he is going to die. The "pit" is synonymous with Sheol, the place for the dead (v. 1). David lifts his hands as he pleads for God's help. His empty hands show utter dependence on God indicating nothing of his own can save him. As he prays toward the holy sanctuary, the place of God's mercy seat, David is relying on God's mercy to save him (v. 2).

As we saw in Psalm 26:9, David asks the Lord not to treat him as if he were one of the wicked who hypocritically hide malice in their hearts. Instead, David entreats the Lord to be just, to repay the wicked for their evil ways, turning their own deeds upon them. Why should God deprive them of mercy? It is because they have disregarded what Yahweh has done. To disregard what the Lord has done is to disregard the Lord himself. Therefore, like a conquering king, Yahweh will destroy them, to be rebuilt never again (v. 5).

In verses 6–7, David realizes the Lord has heard his prayer. He begins saying, "Blessed be the Lord." To pray for God's blessing means asking for his favor, help, and strength, but what does it mean to bless the Lord since he does not need one's favor or any help or added strength? To bless the Lord means to express one's admiration of him and gratitude to him. Consequently, David exclaims the Lord is his strength and protector. When David trusts in God, David receives his help. Therefore, David celebrates and sings to the Lord a song of thanksgiving.

David ends Psalm 28 as he began Psalm 27, declaring that the Lord is a "stronghold." God is the strength and the stronghold of salvation for his people David recognizes that what God is doing is not all about an individual but about a people. Therefore, David prays for the salvation of the people of God, for the Lord to show favor to those who belong to him To "shepherd them" means to provide for them, to guide and protect them. To "carry them" recognizes their weakness and inability to stand or walk on their own and their need for the Lord to get them where he would have them go for eternity (vv. 8–9).

## Living It Out

Psalm 27 and 28 remind us that when our enemies, the world, the flesh, and the devil threaten us, we have a stronghold in the Lord Jesus Christ, our strength and stronghold of salvation. When we put our trust in him and pray, he hears our prayers and helps us. These psalms remind us of how important it is for believers always to seek God's face and faithfully to worship him with other believers. These are the ways God helps us with our struggling perspectives. As we seek the Lord's face and join in corporate worship, we are better equipped to set our "minds on things above" (Col. 3:2).

# The Voice of the Lord

*Psalm 29*

## The Big Picture

[Psalm 29 depicts the awesome supremacy of the Lord over all of his creation as he sits on his throne and reveals his glory with his thunderous voice.] David bears witness to the magnificent display of Yahweh's grandeur and majesty in the midst of a thunderstorm. Nevertheless, this powerful God gives strength and peace to those who trust in him. [The message of Psalm 29 appears to be a refutation of the Canaanite storm god Baal.] The fertility cults of the ancient Near East had many gods that were in some way connected to nature. In Psalm 29, David declares that there is only one God; he is Yahweh, and he sits enthroned in power and majesty over all of nature. Psalm 29 has three sections. Verses 1–2 are a call to worship the Lord, verses 3–9 describe the Lord in the midst of a storm, and verses 10–11 depict Yahweh on his throne.

## Digging In

David begins this psalm repeating the same phrase three times in order to build to a climactic call to worship. When an Old Testament writer repeats a word or phrase three times, it is the writer's way of expressing the greatest emphasis possible, the superlative—the most. The repeated phrase, "Ascribe to the LORD," means to acknowledge Yahweh's attributes and give him what he is due. "Heavenly beings" literally means "sons of God" or "sons of mighty ones." This expression could refer to men of importance. However, the expression also comes from ancient Near Eastern mythology pertaining to the divine assembly, the lesser gods in a pagan pantheon. When the Old Testament writers use this expression pertaining to these gods, it is not affirming the existence of these gods but is instead acknowledging that people believed them to be gods. The expression most likely refers to angels since they are witnesses of God's creation and are constantly ascribing to Yahweh his attributes and glory as they surround his throne (see Ps. 89:6; Job 38:7; Isa. 6:2–3; Ezek. 1). Still, David may be expressing a double entendre here, as the expression would have meant one thing to the pagan nations and another to the people of Israel. He may be taunting the pagans as he commands their gods to submit to Yahweh while at the same time calling out to the angelic host of heaven to worship the Lord.

The phrase "in the splendor of his holiness" has a close connection to the attire of the worshiper and to God's attire. For the worshiper, it means only those who are dressed in Yahweh's holiness may offer him acceptable worship. It is like the priestly attire that signified the Lord had cleansed them of impurities and devoted them to his service. Only those recipients of God's cleansing of sin and those devoted to him are capable of offering worship that is acceptable to God. For the Lord, the expression, "in the splendor of his holiness," refers to Yahweh's royal holy attire. When the prophet Isaiah saw a vision of Yahweh on his throne the Lord's robe filled the temple and the seraphim flew above him calling to one another, "Holy, holy, holy is the LORD of Armies; his glory fills the whole earth" (Isa. 6:3).

Following this call to worship, David describes his experience of seeing God's glory and power over nature in the thunderstorm by focusing on God's voice (Ps. 29:3–9). David mentions God's "voice" seven times in this section. The number seven is significant in the Bible from the very beginning when God completed his work of creation in six days and rested on the seventh. So, the number seven is identified with the idea of being complete or finished. As David speaks of God's voice seven times, he is speaking of God's divine perfection and complete authority to speak and rule over all his creation. He commands nature, and nature obeys his voice.

As angry as the waves of the sea may become in a storm, they are under the Lord's sovereign rule (v. 4). The cedars of Lebanon were known all over the ancient world as the strongest and most impressive trees around as they towered high above all others. Nevertheless, the voice of the Lord not only breaks them but shatters them (v. 5). Mount Sirion is also called Mount Hermon in the Bible as it is today. It is the southernmost extension of the Lebanon mountain range and is the highest point in Israel at an elevation of 9,232 feet above sea level with three summits across the top. Yahweh's voice is so powerful it shakes this mountain range and its most immense mountain in particular like a calf and a young wild ox (v. 6). The lightning of the storm also obeys Yahweh's voice (v. 7). The wilderness, along with all of creation, shakes and trembles with fear upon hearing his voice, and the deer are so startled they give birth prematurely (vv. 8–9a). God's voice lays bare the forests as the angels in the Lord's heavenly temple cry, "Glory!"

Verses 10–11 depict Yahweh on his throne. He is above nature. He will rule over his creation forever, and yet this awesome God enthroned in glory cares for his people, giving them strength and blessing them with peace. [All of nature trembles at the voice of the Lord. However, when the people of the Lord hear his voice, their strength is renewed and they know they are secure.]

## Living It Out

Psalm 29 speaks of the fearful power of God's voice over all creation. But those of us who are believers have every reason to join the angels in ascribing to the Lord glory and strength, worshiping him in the splendor of his holiness. The Lord has forgiven us, cleansed us, and made us holy by the precious blood of Jesus Christ. We are his and he is ours. We do not tremble at his voice. Jesus said, "My sheep hear my voice, I know them, and they follow me. I give them eternal life, and they will never perish. No one will snatch them out of my hand" (John 10:27–28). So, let us join the heavenly host and continually worship our Lord.

# Joy in the Morning

*Psalm 30*

## The Big Picture

Psalm 30 is a psalm of praise. However, the circumstance that precipitated this psalm is ambiguous. The superscription indicates David wrote the psalm for the dedication of the temple, yet some scholars believe this is impossible since David was already deceased when the temple was completed. Nevertheless, 1 Chronicles 22 indicates David did much of the preparations for the building of the temple. Consequently, it is reasonable that David would have written a song in anticipation of its dedication. Additionally, while the superscription indicates the psalm was for the temple dedication, the content of the psalm is quite personal as David exhorts the people to praise the Lord for saving him from an illness that nearly took his life. This happened because God disciplined David for his sinful pride, but then, God saved him. It is possible the people adapted this psalm to their own circumstances as there were numerous times in their history when they experienced God's discipline, which was followed by his compassionate healing and restoration.

## Digging In

David begins the psalm in verses 1–3 praising the Lord for saving him from near-death, for having listened to his cry for help, and for preventing his enemies from having an opportunity to gloat over his demise. The word *lifted* usually refers to drawing water out of a well (Exod. 2:16, 19; Prov. 20:5). Like a bucket submerged into the cold waters in a dark and tight tunnel plunging down into the depths, David was taking his last breaths as he plummeted down until the Lord brought him up from the grips of Sheol, the Pit, the place of the silent dead. As David suffered, he may have wondered if God truly loved him, but when Yahweh, his God, condescended and snatched David from the jaws of death, he was revived as he basked in God's love for him afresh.

David gives God all the credit for his recovery. The Lord heard his cry and healed him. The Lord was his helper and his healer. While the word *healed* usually is in connection with healing from sickness or injury, the context of the remainder of the psalm implies his healing was also spiritual as he received forgiveness for his sin. God was no longer angry with him (Ps. 30:5). Furthermore, David recognized his healing was an answer to his prayer, and his prayer is proof of his trust in the Lord.

Next, David exhorts the people to join him in his song of praise. The "faithful ones" are those who are devoted to the Lord by keeping his covenant through faithful obedience and love for him (v. 4). Singing praises to the Lord is a characteristic of those who are truly faithful to him. The particular reason given for them to praise the Lord is that "his anger lasts only a moment, but his favor, a lifetime" (v. 5). God's last word to his children is never judgment or discipline, and it is always a sign of his love. Proverbs 3:11–12 teaches, "Do not despise the LORD's instruction, my son, and do not loathe his discipline; for the LORD disciplines the one he loves, just as a father disciplines the son in whom he delights" (see Heb. 12:3–12). David knew God's discipline is for the good of his children and lasts for but a moment in light of the eternal joy they experience as God's faithful ones. David acknowledges the difficulty and deep sorrow one experiences while undergoing the

Lord's discipline and anticipates the Lord's favor with the renewal of ⚭ experiencing his love, cleansing, restoration, and blessing.]

Verse 6 indicates what David did to cause God to discipline him. The word *secure* means "at ease" or "prosperous." It appears David's sin was resting in his self-sufficiency. This would be the similar problem Uzziah, one of David's descendants and a future king of Judah, would have. The Scriptures reveal that Uzziah received God's help "until he became strong" (2 Chron. 26:15). This is contrary to God's covenant with Israel: either his people remember that everything they have is a gracious gift of God, or instead, they forget God, take the credit for what they have and perish (Deut. 8:10–18; 30:15–20). David had a similar sense of ease just before he committed adultery with Bathsheba. To be at ease in the Lord is a good thing, but to be at ease in one's own sense of self-accomplishment is an offense to God. David's pride became an obstacle to the success God gave him. It was only when David sensed God's disfavor that he recognized the error of his ways. He was terrified. It was not until he was terrified that David called out to God in repentance for God to save him (vv. 6–8a).

David sought the Lord's favor asking how taking his life would be useful. Would it not be better for the Lord to save him and David proclaim what God has done? So, David asked the Lord to graciously listen to his prayer and help him. David's rhetorical question was his promise to praise the Lord for his salvation, and this psalm is evidence he kept his word (vv. 8b–10). In verses 11–12, David's rejoicing is his response to God's healing him. Sackcloth was what people wore to express grief, but God turned his mourning into dancing so that David could praise the Lord forever.

## Living It Out

Psalm 30 serves as a warning for believers to avoid taking credit for what God has done for them. It is a reminder that the Lord disciplines his children as an expression of his love for them. And even though God's discipline may be difficult to endure, it will not last forever. In fact, it lasts for a very short time in light of spending eternity with him. Psalm 30 also reminds us that God hears and answers the prayers of those who are faithful to him. He heals us of our sins and infirmities. Moreover, the psalm encourages us to remember that our motive for asking God to help us should be so that he will be glorified in it.

# Save Me by Your Faithful Love

*Psalm 31*

## The Big Picture

Psalm 31 is both a lament and a psalm of thanksgiving. Like so many of the previous psalms, it is difficult to know what David's situation was as he wrote this psalm. The psalm has similarities to prayers in the books of Job, Jonah, Jeremiah, and Lamentations. However, while the psalm is a cry for help, it is not altogether clear what kind of help David needed. Verses 1–8 indicate he needed protection from his enemies. Verses 9–12 hint that his problem was physical. Verse 10 suggests that David's troubles may have been because of a sin he committed, and verses 13–18 appear to be a plea for vindication against wrongful accusations. It may have been one thing that precipitated all of these difficulties, or David may have felt overwhelmed by a host of separate issues all at the same time. Whichever it was, David knew he could cry out to God and trust in the Lord to save him, and for this, David was thankful.

## Digging In

David begins Psalm 31 with a plea for God's protection. The words *refuge*, *rock*, and *fortress* convey David's trust in God to shelter him from his enemy's attempt to trap and harm him (vv. 1–4). As in other psalms, David prays he will not be "disgraced," meaning David does not want his faith in God to appear in the eyes of his enemies as misplaced or a mistake. God's action or inaction in this situation not only is a reflection of David but also a reflection on the character of God. David clearly communicates this truth by saying, "you lead and guide me for your name's sake" (v. 3). Therefore, David asks the Lord to save him by the Lord's *"righteousness"* (v. 1). By doing so, the Lord shows the wickedness of David's enemies while at the same time vindicating David's righteousness. David does not try to vindicate himself to his enemies but trusts in God to vindicate him. Moreover, David completely surrenders his life to God, the One who has redeemed him, and the One who is the true God who alone speaks the truth (v. 5).

Consequently, David hates what God hates. To "hate" means to reject and despise. False gods are worthless because they cannot save, but David trusts in Yahweh because he alone can save (v. 6). Therefore, David will rejoice in the Lord's covenantal "faithful love," his *hesed*, since David has already experienced the intimacy of the Lord's faithful love who has seen his affliction and knows what is troubling David. God also has already kept David from the trap of his enemy so far (vv. 7–8).

In verse 9, David renews his plea for God's help and expands upon the nature of his difficulties. David describes the physical suffering that his emotional stress has brought on. He is physically worn out because of the frustration he is experiencing. Tears or just sleepless nights may be the cause of his exhausted eyes, and his weak body may be because he cannot eat or from him being emotionally shaken from the grief he is enduring. To be grieved can mean to be bodily afflicted or endure hardship. David's life has been reduced to grief and groaning as he is bereft of strength and wasting away. Additionally, he is struggling with his own sin nature in the midst of everything (v. 10). He is emotionally, physically, and spiritually spent. To add to David's misery, not only do his adversaries ridicule him but also his friends. They have abandoned him, and they gossip about his demise while his enemy plots to kill him (vv. 11–13). It is such that it is difficult for David to distinguish between his enemies and his friends.

What a difference the word *but* makes in this section of the psalm. It is when David takes his focus off his circumstances, other people, and himself and looks to God that he begins to have a right perspective of his situation. David declares his trust in Yahweh. He can trust in Yahweh because Yahweh is his God. That may seem like an obvious statement, but the truth is that those who do not worship the Lord as their God cannot expect God to save them. One cannot completely disregard and reject the Lord and then expect the Lord to help them out of a tight spot. Only those who are in covenant relationship with him can trust in God's salvation (v. 14).

David submits his circumstances to Yahweh's sovereign control to rescue him from his "persecutors" (v. 15). After that, David declares that his salvation rests on the favor that comes from the Lord's covenant "faithful love." Yahweh's *hesed* is his guarantee to bless his children (v. 16). Next, David prays that the Lord would resolve his predicament—first by vindicating his faith in Yahweh and second by silencing his arrogant enemies with the disgrace they plotted for him. As David closes this section, he recognizes that all of the "righteous" have to contend with these kinds of enemies (vv. 17–18).

Appropriately, verses 19–20 once again contain David's proclamation of God's goodness. God's goodness is all the wonderful things God has for his children. God is known to store up the sins and punishment of the wicked for their day of judgment (Job 21:19; Hos. 13:12; Rom. 2:5). However, since God has stored up goodness for those who fear the Lord, David can expect God's goodness in his situation, and God will display his goodness for all to see, especially for those who take refuge in him. God will receive glory as his very presence protects his children from the measly schemes of mere humans.

David follows up his declaration of God's goodness with praising the Lord one more time. David exclaims his gratitude to and admiration of God as he proclaims, "Blessed be the Lord." The Lord showed his covenant love to David when David was under siege from his enemies.

The Lord also heard his desperate cry and helped him (Ps. 31:20–21). Thus, the Lord vindicated David's faith.

David concludes the psalm with two imperatives to the people of God. The first is, "Love the LORD." This is fundamental to God's covenant with his people. They are to love the Lord their God with all their heart, soul, and strength (Deut. 6:5). This means faithful obedience to Yahweh. Those who arrogantly refuse to obey the Lord will experience his judgment in full (Ps. 31:23). The second imperative is to "Be strong, and let your heart be courageous." True strength and courage is recognizing one's own inadequacy and putting one's "hope in the LORD" (v. 24).

## Living It Out

Psalm 31 encourages believers to hope in the Lord and trust him in spite of all manner of difficulties and challenges in life. However, only those who are believers in the Lord Jesus Christ can trust in his salvation. In this psalm, David reminds us of the strength of prayer and praise as we endure difficulties. Nothing is too difficult for the Lord, and he will be faithful when everyone else seems to have abandoned us. Believers must recognize that we are at our strongest when we recognize our weakness and put our hope in God.

# The Joy of Forgiveness

*Psalm 32*

## The Big Picture

It is possible, David wrote Psalm 32 after he was finally willing to admit his sin of adultery with Bathsheba and the murder of her husband Uriah in 2 Samuel 11–12, with Psalm 32 having a connection to David's confession of these sins in Psalm 51. However, there is no clear indication this is the case. Perhaps, it speaks of another time David sinned. The ambiguity of pinpointing the occasion that precipitated the writing of this psalm allows it more easily to speak to its readers who need to repent and receive the Lord's forgiveness for any number of various sins. Psalm 32 rejoices in the truth that all who confess their sins to God and receive the Lord's gracious forgiveness that leads to restoration will be glad.

## Digging In

The superscription designates Psalm 32 as a *maskil*. This word in Hebrew literally means "enlightened" and is closely connected to teaching and the wisdom literature. This idea fits well with the instruction David gives in Psalm 32.

[Verses 1–2 begin with the theme that carries the message of the entire psalm. One should understand all of the contents of Psalm 32 in light of these opening verses.] Both verses begin with "How joyful!" The reason for this emphatic declaration is that one experiences joy when one receives God's forgiveness. There are four different Hebrew words denoting sin in these verses. *Transgression* means open rebellion against a sacred covenant. Therefore, it is a deliberate act of disloyalty. *Sin* means a failure to meet God's standard of holy behavior. *Iniquity* many times serves as a summary word for all sins personally against God, and *deceit* refers to betrayal and treachery. This list of sins is a comprehensive way of speaking of all sin.

[In verse 1, the word *forgiven* literally means "to be lifted up, to be lifted off, to take away," meaning the Lord lifted up and removed the heavy weight of David's guilt and its penalty from upon him.] The phrase "sin is covered" means God has removed David's sin from out of his sight. He does not look at David as a sinner. In verse 2, the word *charge* is used for keeping accounts or records of funds or to credit or charge to one's account. The same word is used in Genesis 15:6 that states, "Abram believed the LORD, and he [God] credited it to him as righteousness." Here, the picture is of a ledger in heaven that keeps a record of one's sins. David is saying that forgiven sins are permanently erased from the ledger. No matter what the sin is, when God forgives the sin, he has forever put them out of sight and out of mind.

Nevertheless, David did not experience this joy right away. His refusal to immediately confess and repent of his sin to God when he committed his sin cost him the sweet fellowship, he normally experienced with God, causing David to suffer. [When he kept silent about his sin, David discovered that unconfessed sin is like a disease that eats away one's vitality and joy. Saying his bones became brittle communicates how God's disfavor made him a broken man.] Willful rebellion against God brings about a sense of hopelessness and meaninglessness to one who has tasted sweet fellowship with the Lord. Hence, the internal pain of unconfessed sin caused him to groan incessantly. The convicting power of God on David was almost more than he could bear. It is the description of extreme depression as the oppressiveness of his inner turmoil, like a hot, muggy summer day, sapped his strength (vv. 3–4).

His condition changed only when David "acknowledged" his sin, iniquity, and transgressions to the Lord. The word *acknowledged* means that David agreed with God about the egregiousness of his sin. [Confessing sin to God is not informing him of it because God already knows. Confessing sin to God is one's acknowledging one's sin with remorse because of its offensiveness to God.] God would only cover David's sin from his sight when David was willing to cease trying to conceal his sin from God (see v. 1). When David confessed his sin with repentance, God forgave the guilt of his sin. What's more, God took away all the effects of David's sin (v. 5).

[Therefore, David realizes the foolishness of waiting to confess one's sin to God and exhorts "everyone who is faithful" to pray to God immediately for the Lord's forgiveness so that they will not experience what David experienced.] The "faithful" are those who love the Lord and seek faithfully to obey his Word but realize their failings and need for reconciliation with God when they sin. [By not allowing unconfessed sin to linger, they can avoid God's discipline that can rush in suddenly like an overwhelming flash flood (v. 6).] Before they realize it, they can be in over their heads. However, the believer who deals with known sin is immediately and safely hidden from the difficulties that result from unconfessed sin. Instead of being surrounded by the floodwaters of God's discipline, they are surrounded with "joyful shouts of deliverance" (v. 7).

In verses 8–9, David prophetically speaks for the Lord as he watches over the faithful. He instructs believers, counseling them on how they should live. He warns them to avoid being like a horse or mule that has no understanding and therefore needs to be controlled by a bit and bridle to do the will of their master. God will coerce his stubborn children if it is necessary, but his desire is for believers to obey him consciously and willingly because of love for him, not under compulsion from him. If believers act like unbelievers, they will suffer like unbelievers. However, those who trust Yahweh enough to submit to him will experience all the blessings of his covenant love (v. 10).

David concludes his song exhorting the righteous and upright in heart to be glad in the Lord, to rejoice and shout for joy. The righteous and upright in heart are not sinless, but they trust the Lord to forgive their sin as they seek to live for him.

## Living It Out

Psalm 32 reveals the foolishness of believers living with unconfessed sin. While they may not lose their salvation, loss is always the result of sin. Loss of intimacy with Christ, loss of spiritual direction, loss of emotional and physical health are all the results that accompany unconfessed sin. The way to rejoicing is to trust the Lord who gave his life for our sins to mercifully and graciously forgive our sins and cleanse us from all unrighteousness. As we keep short accounts of our sins with God, he completely erases them from our accounts.

# Praise the Creator and King

*Psalm 33*

## The Big Picture

Psalm 33 picks up with the same words Psalm 32 ended: "rejoice, you righteous ones." Therefore, many believe the two psalms were originally connected to one another. If so, it could explain the reason there is no superscription. Along with Psalm 33, only Psalms 1, 2, and 10 have no superscription in this section of the Psalms. Hebrew tradition purports David wrote Psalm 33, but it is impossible to know for sure. After beginning with an exhortation to the righteous to praise the Lord (vv. 1–3), the psalmist provides reasons why they should both praise him (vv. 4–11) and trust in him (vv. 12–19). The psalm concludes with affirmations of faith in the Lord and a request for his "faithful love" to rest on his people (vv. 20–22).

## Digging In

The psalmist begins by calling for the "righteous ones" to "rejoice in the Lord." Moses told the people, "Righteousness will be ours if we are careful to follow every one of these commands before the Lord our God, as he has commanded us" (Deut. 6:25). <u>Therefore, the righteous are those who trust in the Lord and seek to obey him.</u> It is fitting for those who trust and obey the Lord to rejoice in the Lord also because there is no other as trustworthy as the Lord and no other way of life more blessed than one lived in obedience to him.]

The psalmist exhorts his audience to use the instruments of their day and culture to praise the Lord. Musical instruments were an important part of worship. The "lyre" (also called a Kinnor as a transliteration from Hebrew) is the first musical instrument mentioned in the Bible, and David played this instrument. It had anywhere from two to twelve gut strings, was composed of a rectangular or trapezoidal sound box, and was played with a plectrum (a small piece of metal or ivory) or plucked with the fingers. The "ten-stringed harp" was probably the shape of a skin-bottle. These instruments were to accompany the singing of "a new song" to the Lord.[Singing a new song meant identifying with what God has done in the past by singing afresh of his blessings and enjoying his presence anew. The music and joyful shout expressed their passionate praise to God (Ps. 33:2–3).]

Verses 4–5 state the reasons the psalmist insists the righteous praise the Lord. First, Yahweh's word is always upright, faithful, and true. Second, he is reliable to demonstrate his faithful love by his actions. Third, whatever the Lord does is righteous and just, establishing his holiness and wisdom. And finally, Yahweh's covenantal faithful love, his *hesed*, fills the earth. The Lord's "unfailing love" is with his people wherever they go.

In verses 6–9, the psalmist elaborates on how God demonstrated the power of his Word when he created the universe. The heavens and the heavenly hosts were made by God's Word, by "the breath of his mouth." Under the inspiration of the Holy Spirit, the psalmist conveys that the Lord created the world apart from any external forces just by his Word alone just as Genesis 1 reveals. By speaking all of creation into being by his Word, Yahweh reveals his authority over it. Consequently, as chaotic and destructive as the oceans and seas can be with their gigantic waves, hurricanes, and decimating floods, the Lord controls them and stores them as a farmer would his crops. Therefore, the "whole earth" should "fear the LORD" because witnessing such breathtaking power should provoke a sense of "awe of him" as people observe what the Lord is able to do. To "fear the LORD" means having such awe of him it affects how one lives. It precipitates a knowledge of God and leads to a reverence for God, submission to God and the worship of God alone. The apostle John reminds us that Jesus Christ is the word who was with God and was God in the beginning and that he created "all things" (John 1:1–3).

Likewise, Yahweh demonstrates his power and authority over the nations. While he frustrates and thwarts the pretentious designs of human self-rule, the Lord's counsel stands forever, "from generation to generation." The nations' rebellious self-willed plans cannot affect what God is doing. His plans are eternal. Therefore, the nation who belongs to the Lord, submissively lives under his rule, and trusts in his plans will experience God's blessing and favor. God has chosen these people as his treasured possession (Ps. 33:10–12).

Verses 13–17 declare that the Lord observes everything happening on the earth and knows everything everyone is planning and doing because he created them. The greatest sources of protection and power on the earth such as vast armies and weapons cannot save the king who has produced them. The nations depend on military power, but human attempts for self-made security will ultimately fail. Self-reliance is futile. It is only when people recognize their inadequacies that there is hope for them, and the hope of salvation will turn into reality only if they put their trust in God, for he alone can save.

For that reason, as the Lord continually keeps his eye on those who fear him and rest on his faithful love to rescue them from danger and meet their needs, those who fear him have a hope that will come to fruition. The people of God need not fear world powers. However, this hope requires an absolute dependence on God's covenantal faithfulness and love. It necessitates the shredding of self-reliance and self-willfulness and being clothed in submission to Yahweh. God's favor rests on those who fear him (vv. 18–19).

[Furthermore, people of faith wait on the Lord with expectancy. They are convinced of his willingness and ability to help them and defend them in times of need.] Because they have trusted in the holy name of the Lord, they rejoice. His holy name guarantees the blessing of his people. To trust in the name of the Lord is to trust in who he is and what he does. Yahweh's faithful love rests on his covenant people. Therefore, they can put their hope in him and not be disappointed (vv. 20–22).

## Living It Out

There are many reasons believers should praise the Lord, and Psalm 33 reminds us of some of them. It reminds us that we should praise the Lord because by grace through faith in the Lord Jesus Christ we can be called "righteous ones." We should praise God for his Word because it is trustworthy and right and that Jesus Christ is the full expression of the Word of God. Believers should praise the Lord because he is sovereign over the nations. He has chosen to save people from every nation to be his own possession. Moreover, we must remember to praise the Lord because those who expectantly wait on him will be glad they did. ]

# The Lord's Attentive Care for the Righteous

*Psalm 34*

## The Big Picture

The superscription of Psalm 34 indicates the psalm is about David when he was fleeing for his life from King Saul and his soldiers (see 1 Sam. 21). Apparently hoping to blend in, David decided to go to the Philistine city of Gath, ruled by Achish who is also called Abimelech ("my father is king"). It was unlikely Saul would take his soldiers there because the Philistines were Israel's mortal enemies. However, when David approached the city gate, Achish's men recognized David. Fearful they would harm or kill him, David pretended to be crazy, scribbling on doors with spit dripping from his beard. When Achish saw David, he instructed his men to expel David from the city. Upon reading 1 Samuel 21:10–15, one might think David was quite ingenious and shrewd, but Psalm 34 sheds light on how afraid and desperate David was in that moment. David did not rely on his quick thinking and prowess to save him; he depended on the Lord. Psalm 34 is David's testimony of how the Lord attentively cares for the righteous as they trust in him.

## Digging In

Psalm 34 begins with David personally praising the Lord and then calling others to join him as he continues to praise the Lord (vv. 1–3). David exclaims that he will continually express his gratitude and admiration of Yahweh. Emphatically, David proclaims that his life will boast in the Lord and no one else. This is evident with eighteen of the twenty-two verses in the psalm directly referencing the "LORD" by name or by a pronoun. David recognizes his life is in God's hand and that the Lord is the only one who deserves credit for saving David's life. David will incessantly boast in the Lord so that those who have been humbled by some affliction or are impoverished in any way may hear what the Lord did for David and be glad. Their gladness will not only be for David but also for themselves as David's testimony will encourage them with the certainty that God hears and answers the prayers of those who depend on him. Therefore, it makes sense for David to call upon them to join him in proclaiming the "LORD's greatness" and in exalting "his name."

In verses 4–7, David shares his personal testimony of experiencing the Lord's salvation. It is interspersed with appeals to his listeners to look to the Lord also. David's testimony is clear and concise; he "sought the LORD," and the Lord "answered" his prayer and "rescued" him from all his "fears" (v. 4). David's seeking the Lord means David tenaciously prayed to Yahweh for his divine instruction, guidance, and protective care in his time of need. David learned that those who trustingly look to the Lord and fix their gaze on him beam with joy. They will never have any look of disappointment or disillusionment on their faces (v. 5). In verse 6, David repeats his simple yet not simplistic testimony: he humbly "cried," "the LORD heard him," and "saved him from all his troubles." In the Old Testament, "the angel of the Lord" is sometimes identical with Yahweh and at other times distinct from him, but he always foreshadows the person and work of the Lord Jesus Christ. David recognizes the Lord is the Divine Warrior encamped with his people, fighting for them.

In verse 8, David challenges his hearers to taste and see if what he is saying about the Lord is true. They must judge for themselves the accuracy of what David is saying, and in order to experience God's goodness, they will need to abandon any vestiges of self-sufficiency and trust in him alone. They may have never experienced the joy of answered prayer. James speaks to this point saying, "You do not have because you do not ask" (James 4:2). "His holy ones," those whom God has chosen to be his treasured possession and be devoted to him must "fear the Lord," having an awe-filled reverence for God, submitting to his will, and worshiping him alone. When they do this, they will lack nothing because God is responsive to their needs. Even those young lions that are most adept at hunting may occasionally lose their prey and go hungry, but those who seek Yahweh will always receive what is best for them (Ps. 34:10). Why? Ultimately, it is because those who seek the Lord will find him, and he is the greatest of all treasures.

In verses 11–14, David teaches what fearing the Lord involves. If a person wants to live a long enjoyable life, then he or she needs to do the following: 1) One must keep one's tongue from speaking in a way that offends the Lord or is injurious to others. It means what one says must be true, helpful, inspirational, necessary, and kind. 2) One needs to shun what is offensive to God and do what is pleasing to God by obeying his Word (see Deut. 5:29; 1 Tim. 1:8). And 3) make every effort to intentionally and actively pursue peace. This includes peace with God, with others, and within.

David is realistic about the life of a believer. The righteous have "many adversities," but the Lord watches over the righteous and responds to their cries for help. Unlike the wicked whom the Lord will remove from memory, the Lord is especially sensitive to the cries of those with broken and contrite hearts and is always ready to save them. They are not alone. Those "crushed in spirit," the ones discouraged, can trust God to save. He protects those who belong to him (Ps. 34:15–20). Conversely, the unrepentant wicked ones who hate the people of God will suffer the wages of their sin, death (v. 21). However, "the Lord redeems the life of his servants," meaning the Lord will treat those who trust in him as if they had never sinned (v. 22).

## Living It Out

Psalm 34 should remind believers of a number of things. We should remember to give God the credit for everything he has done for us. Apart from him, we can do nothing. Believers must be diligent to share with others what God has done for them. God blesses us not only for our sake, but for the sake of encouraging other believers to recognize that God also has blessed them and will continue to bless them. We must never underestimate the power of our testimony to be a blessing to others. Additionally, this psalm teaches that a life lived for God involves what we say, what we do, and how we relate to God and others. However, above all else, Psalm 34 should remind us that God meets all of our needs and that these needs ultimately are met in the person and work of the Lord Jesus Christ.

# A Prayer to the Divine Warrior

*Psalm 35*

## The Big Picture

Psalm 35 is a lament with David expressing his need for God to fight for him against his enemies. It also has elements of an imprecatory psalm in it. An imprecatory psalm is one where the psalmist asks God to cause harm and destruction to his enemies. These psalms convey a yearning for God's justice for atrocities committed against the people of God. Under the inspiration of the Holy Spirit, the writers of imprecatory psalms are not simply asking for revenge but instead are asking for God to keep his promise of divine vengeance against those who abuse his people. In Deuteronomy 32:35, God said, "Vengeance belongs to me; I will repay." Lest one think it is only "the God of the Old Testament" who makes these kinds of statements as if God in the Old Testament is somehow different from God in the New Testament, note the words of Paul: "Friends, do not avenge yourselves; instead, leave room for God's wrath, because it is written, 'Vengeance belongs to me; I will repay,' says the Lord" (Rom. 12:19). Moreover, the Lord Jesus Christ said, "Will not God grant justice to his elect who cry out to him day and night? Will he delay helping them? I tell you that he will swiftly grant them justice" (Luke 18:7–8a). ◀

Today, believers must recognize the New Testament reveals their enemies as not physical but spiritual (Eph. 6:12). People who oppose the kingdom of God are secondary agents and are under the influence of the primary enemies of God. The primary enemies of God and believers are the devil, the world, and the flesh (John 14:30; 1 John 2:15; Gal. 5:17), and it is right for believers to pray for their defeat and God's justice. God's Word indicates he will finally defeat and eradicate them (Rev. 19:2). When one prays with a concern for God's glory and the salvation of his people and not for one's personal comfort or sense of vindictiveness, these prayers uphold the heart and purposes of God. ✦

## Digging In

The first section of Psalm 35, verses 1–10, begins with a cry to Yahweh to intervene both legally and militarily on his behalf. The word *oppose* is a legal term, and David uses it to ask the Lord to come to his legal defense and show that David is innocent of any action that would merit his enemy's onslaught against him. Next, David asks the Lord to fight for him. David was not asking the Lord to do anything he had not been willing to do for God. When David faced Goliath, he told the Philistine, "I come against you in the name of the LORD of Armies . . . you have defied him. . . . I'll strike you down. . . . Then all the world will know that Israel has a God . . . for the battle is the LORD's" (1 Sam. 17:45–47).

Now in this precarious situation, David needs reassurance that the Lord is his salvation, that Yahweh will act on David's behalf (Ps. 33:3). Helpless before his enemies, David prays that the Lord will disgrace, humiliate, repulse, shame, drive away, and bring to ruin with their own traps those who have sought to harm him (vv. 4–8). In the center of these requests, David emphasizes that what his enemies are doing to him is "without cause" (v. 7). In other words, he is innocent of any wrongdoing. David concludes this section anticipating the Lord's deliverance and promising to praise God for saving David from enemies that are "too strong for him" (vv. 9–10).

In verses 11–16, David expresses his sense of betrayal. His enemies are people to whom David had shown kindness. He showed concern for them by putting on sackcloth (an outward sign of grief), by fasting (a sign of continual concern), and by praying for them with the same fervor he would for his dearest loved ones if they were physically afflicted (vv. 13–14). Despite this, these friends he cared for were unreliable and betrayed David. They rejoiced when David experienced trouble, and their ridicule and slander were so shocking that his so-called friends were unrecognizable. They were not the people he had known them to be (vv. 15–16). It is for these cruelties David wonders how long God can watch without doing anything about it. He pleads with the Lord to restore him from these powerfully dangerous enemies and save the only thing he has left to him, his life (v. 17). As with the first part of the psalm, David concludes this section by counting on God to save him, this time so that David will be able to exalt the Lord "among many people" (v. 18).

In the final section of Psalm 35, David prays for God's vindication. He petitions his righteous God to deal with David's treacherous enemies who twist the truth and rejoice when he is in trouble. To "wink" at him "maliciously" means to act and speak with duplicity with the intent of harming David (v. 19). Nevertheless, David knows the Lord has seen everything that has transpired, and is therefore confident the Lord will rise up to his defense because God is his Master and Lord. David is confident the Lord comes to the defense of those who are hated "without cause" and who "live peacefully in the land."

David's request for the Lord to vindicate him is more about God's reputation than it is about David's personal difficulties. It is about the Lord his God and his righteousness. By keeping with his own righteousness, the Lord demonstrates that he can be trusted to be righteous and do what is right. David is declaring that he knows God is righteous and therefore always knows what is right and always does what is right (v. 24).

Consequently, David prays that his enemies will not have the last word in the matter. It is because the Lord will not remain silent that David knows his enemies will be silenced. The Lord will disappoint their wicked designs for the child of God and they will be "clothed with shame and reproach," as God's justice is served (vv. 25–26).

David's last words reveal that he recognizes there are others like him who long for vindication and God's justice. He exhorts them to rejoice in the truth that the Lord "takes pleasure in his servant's well-being." Therefore, David declares he will proclaim the righteousness of God and praise him "all day long" (vv. 27–28).

## Living It Out

Psalm 35 reveals a number of truths believers need to remember. First, in difficult times, even those with strong faith in the Lord sometimes need reassurance that they can trust the Lord to answer their prayers. Sometimes he delivers them out of difficulty, and at other times, God delivers them through the difficulty, but he is always with them. Second, like David, the Lord Jesus Christ understands betrayal and knows how his children feel when their friends have betrayed them. Third, be a true friend to others as Jesus is our true friend. Fourth, it is important to remember to praise God when he answers prayer. And finally, believers must realize that even in the darkest times of sorrow, the Lord takes pleasure in the well-being of those who serve him. One can never out-serve the Lord.

# Human Wickedness and Divine Lovingkindness

*Psalm 36*

## The Big Picture

Psalm 1 confronts the reader with "two ways," the way of the wicked and the way of the righteous. The way of the wicked is a meaningless life of ungodliness that ultimately leads to destruction. In contrast, the way of the righteous is a blessed life that glorifies God. Psalm 36 revisits the certainties of Psalm 1 by contrasting the way of the wicked with the faithful love of Yahweh. Psalm 36 has four sections. The first is an analysis of the transgressions of the wicked (vv. 1–4). Conversely, the second describes the faithful, loving-kindness of God to those who trust in him (vv. 5–9). The third section is David's prayer for Yahweh to continue caring for him (vv. 10–11), and the last section is the final verse, declaring David's confidence in the ultimate downfall of the wicked (v. 12). As Psalm 1 does, David once again confronts the reader of Psalm 36 with two ways from which to choose: the way that leads to destruction or the way of life.

## Digging In

In the superscription of Psalm 36, David is called "the LORD's servant" or literally "the servant of the LORD." A servant is someone who does the will of another. The idea of the Lord's servant appears in a number of places with God referring to about fifteen people as his servant. However, of the twenty-two times this distinct title, "the Servant of the LORD," appears in the Old Testament, seventeen of them refer to Moses, two to Joshua, two to David, and one to Israel in Isaiah 42:19. This title of "the Servant of the LORD" is the designation of one who has a particular position with the purpose of representing Yahweh to others. God called Moses, Joshua, and David to represent him and speak to the people of God on his behalf, since Israel was called to be a kingdom of priests and represent Yahweh to the nations. It is therefore no surprise given Jesus is God, the actual flesh-and-blood representation of God, that Isaiah points to Christ as the Servant of the LORD. Moreover, Jesus identifies himself as a servant, and the New Testament writers affirm this truth.

Psalm 36 begins with "an oracle." *Oracle* is a technical term referring to the proclamation of a prophet who preached divine revelations to Israel. One might question if David truly was a prophet, but at the end of his life, David said, "The Spirit of the LORD spoke through me, his word was on my tongue" (2 Sam. 23:2). What's more, in Acts 2:30–31, Peter asserts David was a prophet who foretold Jesus' resurrection. In Psalm 36, David recognizes his role as a prophet and servant of the Lord, revealing with authority the insights given him under the inspiration of the Holy Spirit.

David both witnessed the ways of the wicked and received insight into their thoughts and motivations from God. The "wicked" are unbelievers who have never repented of their sin, who live in rebellion against God, and have never placed their faith in him. Not only do these people not "fear the Lord" such as the righteous do with overwhelming awe, holy reverence, willing submission, and joyful worship of God, but they do not even recognize the dreadful consequences of their unbelief and rebellion against God. They are about to fall off a high cliff with absolutely no perception or appreciation of their perilous situation. In their opinion, there is no need to fear God (v. 1). What blinds the eyes of the wicked to their sin and its hideousness? It is their high opinion of themselves (v. 2). In their eyes, arrogance is a prized character quality. However, the apostle Paul warns believers not to think of oneself more highly than one should think but to think sensibly, with an honest evaluation of oneself (Rom. 12:3). Additionally, the motive of the wicked as they speak is to cause others pain while deceiving them. The idea of doing what they were taught to be good is foolish to them (Ps. 36:3). Therefore, their rejection of what they once knew was good has led them to embrace evil. Their dismissive perception of God, in their thinking, has led to plans that will harm others and are contrary to the way of the Lord (v. 4). Their spiritually blinded condition may cause them and others like them to think what they are doing is good, but anything that fails to acknowledge the Lord is evil in his eyes.

In verses 5–9, David expresses his praise to God for God's goodness. David highlights four limitless characteristics of the Lord by which he preserves life: his faithful love, his faithfulness, his righteousness, and his judgments. Yahweh's "faithful love" is his *hesed*, Yahweh's expression of his covenant with his people to bless them with his tender care, his abundant provision, and strong protection. Such faithful love is refreshing and priceless. God's "faithfulness" means he is consistent in his character, trustworthy, and dependable. The Lord's "righteousness" means that he is perfect in every way and is the standard of what is right, good, and proper. Akin to God's righteousness is his "judgments." God's judgments are the decisions he makes that are righteous and as unfathomable as the "deepest sea." Yahweh is both the source and Sustainer of all life. Moreover, unlike the spiritually blind, a life lived unto God is an enlightened life as God sheds his light into the hearts and minds of believers.

David follows these words of praise with a short petition for God's protection in verses 10–11. David calls upon the Lord's covenant faithful love to continue to protect the people of God from those who are arrogant, the wicked. David prays to the God of righteousness to protect the upright, those whom God has declared righteous because of their faith in God. David goes to the One he acknowledges as the source of life to save the lives of his people by driving away the wicked.

In verse 12, David concludes his prophetic oracle with a vision of the downfall of the wicked. His vision serves as an exhortation for believers to trust in God's salvation. It also serves as a warning. There are two ways to live one's life. The way of the wicked will ultimately lead to destruction, never to rise again, but the way of the upright is a "wellspring of life" (v. 9).

## Living It Out

Psalm 36 should remind believers that when they have too high an opinion of themselves they are like the wicked and are more likely to ignore the conviction of the Holy Spirit and overlook sin in their lives. Given that the wicked are unaware of their iniquity and consequently do not hate it, it is safe to conclude that in contrast, the righteous are aware of their sin and loathe it. Like David, we should acknowledge and praise God for the immensity and impressiveness of his faithful love, faithfulness, righteousness, and judgments toward us. In like manner, let us also pray for the continuing experience of God's faithful love.

# Instruction in Wisdom

*Psalm 37*

## The Big Picture

Psalm 37 is an acrostic psalm in Hebrew with each section beginning with a consecutive letter of the alphabet. The occasion of its writing is unknown, but sounding much like the book of Proverbs, it is a wisdom psalm of David where later in his life he gives counsel to those who may be agitated or fearful, especially because of evildoers. The plans, prosperity, and even the existence of evildoers in a world where God reigns can be perplexing. Nevertheless, David's exhortation is that the commitment of believers needs to be a calm confidence, remaining faithfully obedient to the Lord, trusting in his wisdom and power to deal with the wicked in his perfect timing and way. Most assuredly, those who take refuge in the Lord will be protected in the present and enjoy an ongoing future. However, Psalm 37 elaborates on the last verse of Psalm 36 which states, "The evildoers have fallen. They have been thrown down and cannot rise." Similarly, Psalm 37 encourages beleaguered believers to remember that the wicked, with their threats and prosperity, are temporary and one day will perish.

## Digging In

Psalm 37 begins with an exhortation for believers not to fret over those who do evil. No matter how much it may appear they are thriving, their end is certain. In ancient Israel, the grass sprouted lushly green in the spring, but it only took one dry, oppressively hot wind for it to wilt away. Likewise, the wicked may appear to prosper, but their threats to the righteous and personal successes will be short-lived. Therefore, it is unwise to be "agitated" by them or to "envy" them (vv. 1–2).

Instead of concerning oneself with these temporary perplexities, as aggravating as they can be, the believer must have an eternal perspective by trusting in the Lord to do what is right and faithfully obeying him. Faithful obedience to God is evidence of trusting in him. It is the result of hoping in God's faithfulness to do what is right. Taking "delight in the LORD" means adoring and esteeming the Lord far beyond anyone or anything else. It means enjoying intimacy with him as loving Father and dearest friend. It means joyfully worshiping and thanking him for who he is, what he has done, and what he has promised. Therefore, those who take "delight in the LORD" will receive their heart's desire because they realize the Lord is their greatest treasure, and their heart's desire will be the Lord himself (vv. 3–4).

The word *commit* in verse 5 literally means "to roll." Therefore, it asserts believers need to turn over their whole lives, their desires, jealousies, problems, resentment, and fears over to the Lord. The Lord responds to the faith of his people, and his response will be an extraordinary reversal. The righteousness and justice of his people will suddenly appear and brilliantly shine as the Lord vindicates them for trusting in him (v. 6). Accordingly, believers silently and expectantly should wait on the Lord without complaint, cries of anguish, or outbursts of anger. Such emotional upheavals will only cause them more harm. Instead, those who put their hope in the Lord are assured of an inheritance of abundant blessing from the Lord, while the wicked will be no more (vv. 7–11).

Verses 12–15 describe the wicked. They have schemes plotting to ruin and ultimately kill those faithful to Yahweh (see v. 32). The gnashing of their teeth may mean their intent is to intimidate and antagonize believers, or it could mean the wicked have such loathing for believers that the very thought of believers causes the wicked to gnash their teeth. [Reminiscent of the arrogant kings who conspire "against the LORD and his Anointed One" (2:2), the wicked also are the brunt of the Lord's mocking laughter because he knows their "day is coming," a day of destruction.]The wicked are poised to strike the poor and needy and slaughter believers, but their weapons will be turned against them and pierce their own hearts. They are greedy and cursed enemies of God who in the end will destroy them (vv. 20, 22, 38).

Consequently, believers should be content with what they have. Because of the fate of the wicked, having a little is better than the brief time of prosperity they may enjoy. Like one with broken arms who cannot defend oneself, the wicked will be powerless before the Lord. Conversely, the Lord will support and watch over believers; their inheritance will last forever. Because he takes pleasure in the way of those who delight in him, he will protect them and provide for them in difficult times (vv. 16–19, 23–24, 33).

What's more, over the many years of his life, David never witnessed God abandon his faithful ones, and he observed that they and their children have always been generous to others (vv. 25–26). Therefore, believers should shun evil and do what is good. In addition, those who are truly righteous speak words of wisdom because the Word of God is in their heart, providing them sure footing for life (vv. 30–31). They faithfully obey the Lord with expectancy, looking to God's justice and their vindication. No matter how invulnerable the wicked appear, a time will come when there will not even be evidence they ever existed (vv. 34–36, 38).

David concludes with some final words of exhortation and encouragement for believers. First, it is wise to watch godly believers to learn from their examples as they expectantly and peacefully hope in the Lord. This is the path to eternal life because the Lord is their refuge and they trust in his salvation. Moreover, the Lord will always save those who recognize their utter helplessness and place their faith in him (vv. 37, 39–40). David's message to unbelievers is that they are on the path to destruction unless they turn away from evil and turn to God. The Lord's message to believers is that they need to trust in him, faithfully obey him, and expectantly look for the day when he will vindicate their faith in him.

## Living It Out

David points out several truths we must embrace. We must not allow the temporary prosperity and the seeming upper hand of unbelievers to make us anxious, jealous, or angry. Instead, we need to trust in God's wisdom to deal with them in his good time, knowing that he will. Also, wisdom comes from the Lord through his Word. It is knowing God's Word and living by his Word that keeps us from faltering. God takes pleasure in those who are faithful to him. Instead of complaining to the Lord by focusing on the wicked we need to turn our attention to our Lord and Savior Jesus Christ and experience the rich blessing of knowing him. What's more, as we serve the Lord we can patiently wait on him inevitably to make everything right because he is faithful to keep his promises.

# A Prayer of Confession

*Psalm 38*

## The Big Picture

The weight of sin and its consequences in the life of a believer can seem excruciating. The writer of the book of Hebrews wrote, "The Lord disciplines the one he loves and punishes every son he receives. . . . No discipline seems enjoyable at the time, but painful. Later on, however, it yields the peaceful fruit of righteousness to those who have been trained by it" (Heb. 12:6, 11). In Psalm 38, David recalls a time in his life when he suffered because of God's displeasure with David's sin. The occasion or sin that precipitated the psalm is unknown, but the superscription of the psalm indicates it is a psalm "to bring remembrance." It may have been written either in order for God to remember what was happening or for David to remember what happened. In ancient Israel, to ask God to "remember" was an expression that in reality was asking God to take action. This idea certainly fits the contents of this psalm. On the other hand, perhaps David wrote it so that he could actually remember the valuable lesson he learned from the experience of his sin, its consequences, and God's forgiveness. Most likely, the expression "to bring remembrance" refers to God, but David, no doubt, wrote the psalm so that he would be reminded of what happened and so that he could instruct and encourage others by it as well. Psalm 38 is a lament that touches upon the themes of divine discipline, suffering, sin, guilt, confession, and hope in God's salvation.

## Digging In

Bible teachers and students alike are divided on whether or not to take David's description of his condition literally or figuratively. If taken literally, then David describes his suffering from some serious illness that was a consequence of his own sin. If taken figuratively, then these verses depict the emotional sorrow and psychological distress that pressed down upon him as he lived with his sin and endured the heaviness of God's discipline. The most natural reading is to understand it as a poetic description of a genuine illness without undervaluing the emotional pain that certainly accompanied his physical suffering. Whatever David's infirmity is, God uses it to open his eyes to his spiritual condition and lead him to confession and repentance.

Not all sickness and suffering is the result of personal sin, but David realizes that in this instance his illness is God's discipline for sin. In this way, David acknowledges his sin. In verse 1, the Lord's "anger" and "wrath" speak of God's righteous judgment against his enemies. David's cry is for God mercifully to treat him like a son, not as an enemy. The words *punish* and *discipline* both denote punishment accompanied by correction and instruction.

Following his initial plea for mercy, David describes his suffering. In the ancient Near East, it was common for people to think of illnesses as arrows shot from a deity. Additionally, God's "hand" is an ancient Israelite way of referring to his power. Therefore, David recognizes his affliction is from the powerful hand of God (v. 2). What's more, the effects of his condition is all consuming with his entire body affected because of God's indignation at David's sin (v. 3). David's sin is like a flood that threatens to drown him, and his guilt is more than he can bear. His disease manifests itself with foul-smelling infectious sores, and he realizes it is the consequence of his foolishness, his sin. Foolishness in the Bible is disregarding God and choosing to go one's own way, and it is a profound way of describing sin. David's searing pain in his abdominal region has him bent over, faint, and crushed as he spends his day weeping and groaning over his physical and spiritual condition (vv. 4–8).

In verses 9–11, recognizing that because of his sin God is disciplining him and his condition is certainly known by God, as his body continues to deteriorate, David expresses his desire for God to mercifully forgive and heal him. His condition is so bad that even his friends and loved ones are distancing themselves from him. It may be that they are repulsed by what they witness and smell, or it may be that they too recognize this as God's discipline and therefore hope to avoid guilt by association. Either way, their abandonment coupled with God's discipline is unbearable.

Adding to his agony, his enemies are trying to capitalize on his weakened, vulnerable state by slandering him and scheming to eliminate him. They are opportunists who seek to exacerbate his suffering. They are like hyenas ready to pounce on some poor injured or wounded prey. David is so stunned and overwhelmed by it all that he is too numb to hear what people are saying. In addition, he is unable to say anything. It has become all too much for him. David's enemies are formidable and attack him because of his devotion to serve the Lord. In reality, nothing his enemies plot against him is able to add to his misery because David is already at the end of his rope. The only thing he can do is hope in Yahweh, his Master and God, to save him and vindicate him before his enemies. For this reason, David confesses his iniquity but is concerned about sinning again in the future. His confession is not only about getting a quick fix in his immediate situation but an expressed desire to be devoted to God going forward (vv. 12–20).

In verses 21–22, David concludes with three requests while addressing God in three different ways. The first request is for Yahweh, his personal covenant God, not to abandon him. In other words, David is asking the Lord to make his manifest presence perceptible to David. Second, David calls the Lord, "my God." The Hebrew word for "God," "*Elohim*," recalls the God who is the Creator, Sustainer, and Judge of his creation, infinite in power and wisdom. This is David's God, and David is asking his God to attend to his needs. And the third request is to his "Lord," or master. David is declaring his devotion to God and his recognition that the Lord is his salvation. Therefore, as a servant of the Lord, David trusts his master to act quickly given the urgency of the situation.

## Living It Out

Psalm 38 reminds believers we should not take our sin lightly. It highlights the dire consequences of sin. Our loving heavenly Father will discipline us for our good, even though experiencing his discipline can be very difficult. He disciplines his children to keep them from harm and to help them grow into the image of his Son, the Lord Jesus Christ. It should remind us that God's relationship to his children is both personal and powerful to answer our prayers and save us in times of need. We must refuse to conceal our sin. Instead, we need to keep short accounts with God by repenting and confessing our sin to him as soon as possible.

# The Brevity of Life

*Psalm 39*

## The Big Picture

Like Psalm 38, the occasion of Psalm 39 cannot be determined, but it also is a psalm of lament by David during a difficult time of God's discipline for David's sin. In fact, Psalm 39 is the last of a trio of psalms that mirror three of the books in the wisdom literature of the Old Testament. Psalm 37 has the precepts and instruction of Proverbs, Psalm 38 depicts a struggle similar to Job, and Psalm 39 contemplates the brevity of life and its meaning much like the Preacher does in Ecclesiastes. All three psalms maintain a steadfast hope in the Lord as David struggles with his enemies. David comes to terms with the frailty and brevity of life in Psalm 39 and realizes his only hope in life is in the Lord. David prays that the Lord would remove his discipline so that David might enjoy the short time he has left on the earth.

## Digging In

The superscription specifies this psalm is "for the choir director, for Jeduthun." The superscriptions of Psalms 62 and 77 also mention

Jeduthun which is probably another name for Ethan. First Chronicles 16:41 indicates Jeduthun was one of David's chief musicians. He was one of three choir directors David appointed to lead the people of God in worship at the temple.

Verses 1–3 introduce David's situation, his suffering and his struggle to keep silent in front of unbelievers. It is impossible to know for certain what he was keeping to himself, but whatever it was, he realized it would have been wrong to say, especially in front of the wrong people. Either he was concerned about being misunderstood in a way that might encourage the wicked or he was possibly embittered inside against God for his state of affairs and his heated complaining would have dishonored God. The statements, "My heart grew hot within me" and "as I mused, a fire burned" both appear to communicate that the more he thought about it the angrier he got. In Hebrew, the idiom for becoming angry is to get "hot." If David had expressed his anger at God or at anyone else for that matter because of his ordeal, his enemies would have been delighted to witness such a tirade. The wicked are always looking for an opportunity to rejoice and taunt believers for their failings. David's silence demonstrated his loyalty to God by refusing to give the wicked fuel to mock God. Furthermore, even when David thought about saying something positive, his pain got worse.

However much David tried to be silent, he finally was compelled to speak. In verses 4–6, David expressed his thoughts about the frailty and brevity of his life. He prayed that God would help him live with an awareness of his mortality. He recognized that compared to his eternal God, David's life is but inches long. As David's son Solomon observed in Ecclesiastes, David perceived human life is like a vapor one breathes on a chilly morning that appears and quickly disappears. The Hebrew word translated "vapor" in verse 5 is translated as "absolute futility" in Ecclesiastes 1:2. Used with "shadow," it emphasizes the brevity of life. However, the Hebrew word for vapor is *hebel*, and it means more than just a short time. This word is the root word for "Abel" who was murdered by his brother Cain (Gen. 4:8). This incident of a life cut short and the futility of it is at the center of meaning for this word. David expounded on this idea in verse 6 as he described the meaninglessness of accumulating material wealth without recognizing, that with death, someone else will have it all. David observed that life is short and futile.

Perhaps verses 4–6 provide some clue as to what David could not say in verses 1–3. Conceivably, he had trouble understanding the benefit of the wicked soon being gone if he will soon be dead himself (see Ps. 37:35–36). What's more, if everyone's life is short, then would it not be better to have a short-lived life of prosperity like the wicked rather than have no prosperity at all and live a life of misery? Also, what is the real profit in disciplining one whose lifespan is so brief? Maybe David was continuing to struggle understanding these things.

In verse 7, two words bring an abrupt halt to David's dark thoughts and perplexing questions: "Now, Lord." He uses the word *Lord*, meaning "Master." No matter what his difficulties were, David was loyal to his Master. Therefore, he waits on the Lord with hope. It is a declaration of a faith that expectantly hopes in God with enduring patience. There is no one else he can turn to and no one else he would rather turn to. David's affirmation of his hope in God is at the center of this psalm and at the heart of its meaning. David finally has a proper perspective on life. When believers struggle in the midst of God's chastening and are surrounded by unbelievers, God is their only hope, and those who hope in him will not be disappointed. What David knows about God outweighs what he fails to comprehend about everything else. Whether or not we can make sense of what is happening, God always does.

Therefore, David asks the Lord to forgive him and remove the consequences of his sin. This will be the only way David can be healed since his sins are the reason for his affliction. Deliverance from the consequences of sin will only come from confession of sin in repentance and faith. David wants to honor God with his life. Unanswered prayer and his continuing in such a sorry state would only bring dishonor to God before his enemies. Only the Lord's favor is able to deliver one from his disfavor (v. 8). David recognizes his sin and silently refrains from arguing against God's justice. What tormented him most was the rift in his relationship with God. His only words are cries for God's merciful forgiveness and restoration. For this reason, with tears, he concludes the psalm with a final plea for God's deliverance. His consuming desire is once again to enjoy intimacy with God before his life is over (vv. 9–13).

## Living It Out

Psalm 39 highlights the importance of recognizing what we say has consequences and that believers show their loyalty to God and concern for others when they are mindful of what comes out of their mouths. Believers must be aware that the wicked are always looking for an opportunity to rejoice and taunt believers for their failings. Psalm 39 also demonstrates there is no contradiction between having questions and having faith when one takes their questions to God and his Word. When we do, we are reminded just as David was that what we know about Christ outweighs everything else we do not understand. Finally, intimacy with Christ should be treasured above all else, for only Jesus can satisfy our souls.

# Thanksgiving and the Need for Continued Help

*Psalms 40–41*

## The Big Picture

Psalm 40 begins with David thanking Yahweh for hearing and answering his prayer for help. God vindicated David's trust in him, so in light of this, David proclaims his continued devotion to the Lord. At the same time, even though the Lord delivered David in the past, David continued to struggle with difficulties. For this reason, the second half of Psalm 40 contains a lament with David, once again, crying out to God for a speedy deliverance from his enemies (vv. 11–17). Most of this section is repeated in the book of Psalms as Psalm 70. Psalm 41 is yet another lament where David indicates he is in poor health and his enemies are attempting to take advantage of him in his time of weakness. It is also a graphic description of David's sense of estrangement and betrayal by a friend. Nevertheless, David realizes he can always trust in the Lord because the Lord who is eternal delights in his children. The occasions for both Psalms 40 and 41 are unknown, making their truths more readily accessible to all who read them, and they conclude the first of five books that make up the Psalms.

## Digging In

Verses 1–3 in Psalm 40 describe how God saved David in his time of need. The phrase, "I waited patiently," is emphatic in its original Hebrew language, and it expresses intensity and perhaps David's difficulty he had waiting expectantly on the Lord. Nonetheless, God listened to David's cry for help and eventually bent down to David. It is an expressive picture of a loving Father caring for his child. Both Joseph and the prophet Jeremiah experienced being thrown into a pit by their enemies (Gen. 37:24; Jer. 38:6). Therefore, it is not beyond the realm of possibility David is speaking literally. Then again, it is just as possible that David is speaking figuratively to describe the dire straits he was in. Either way, the grimness of his situation is the point (Ps. 26:1).

All things considered, the Lord wonderfully saved David and set his feet on a safe and stable foundation. Furthermore, God put "a new song" in David's mouth. The Lord gave David yet another reason to thank God and praise him. Moreover, David's declarations of praise will be an encouragement to others who will see what God did, fear him in awe, and consequently put their trust in him (vv. 2–3). In verses 4–5, David declares God vindicates those who put their trust in the Lord by asserting they will be happy for having done so. Then, David recognizes nothing, and no one compares with God, the wondrous things he has done, and the wonderful things he has planned for his people.

Verses 6–8 explain what is most pleasing to God. God is not interested in mere acts of worship. Rather, he is most interested in the reality of what their sacrifices and offerings represent. For instance, the burnt offering represented a desire to renew a right relationship with God and express total devotion to him. The sin offering was for the cleansing of sins. These acts of worship mean nothing to God if they were not an accurate expression of what was in the heart of the worshiper. These expressions of worship only have meaning when the ones offering them listen to God's Word and faithfully obey it in love and devotion to

God. Ultimately, the significance of these Old Testament sacrifices is in anticipation of the only true acceptable sacrifice for one's sins, the death of Christ on the cross (Heb. 10:5–10).

Likewise, the person who authentically lives for the Lord will follow David's example when he says, "I do not keep my mouth closed" (v. 9). True believers will openly testify to the Lord's "faithfulness and salvation," and will not "conceal" God's "constant love and truth" from others, especially from other believers who also need a word of encouragement (v. 10). In verse 11, David expresses his complete confidence in the Lord to "always guard" him. David's memory of God's faithfulness to deliver David in the past gives him confidence God will continue to do the same now and in the future.

The remaining part of the psalm is David's cry for help. In this instance, the cause of the troubles that have "overtaken" him is his own sin, and they have become physically, emotionally, and spiritually overwhelming to him (v. 12). During this struggle, David's enemies are trying to exploit it and destroy him. He asks the Lord to shame them, confuse them, repel them, utterly defeat them, and cause them to be appalled by all of it (vv. 13–15). On the contrary, David prays that all who seek the Lord will have reason to rejoice in his salvation and greatness (v. 16). David concludes Psalm 40 humbly admitting his need and asking the Lord to consider him and his plight. David confidently declares the Lord is his "helper" and "deliverer." Nevertheless, his current struggle causes him to implore God not to delay (v. 17).

Psalm 41 is closely connected to Psalms 38–40, all of which reveal times of suffering in David's life. In this instance, once again his suffering was some sort of sickness that was the result of sin in his life (v. 4). The psalm has three parts. Verses 1–3 introduce the psalm with words of instruction and promised blessing to those who heed the instruction. The message is straightforward: God will help and protect those who help others who are in need. In verses 4–9, David confesses his sin and asks for God's gracious healing. Also, David describes how his enemies anticipate his demise and how even a trusted friend has betrayed him. In verses 10–12, David prays that God will heal him so that he can bring his enemies to justice. David knows the Lord delights in David's devotion to God and therefore will support him in this matter. To conclude, verse 13 serves as a doxology and benediction to the first book of the Psalms composed of Psalms 1–41.

## Living It Out

Everyone should be confident that God is able to save people who are in trouble, even the deepest trouble, and give them security and reason to praise him. It also is essential for believers to share with others their testimony of how God has saved them so that others might come to trust in the Lord. It is part of God's design to use believers as witnesses and instruments of blessing to others. Unlike the saying, "God helps those who help themselves," Psalm 41 teaches that God helps those who are actively helping others. Praising God not only blesses the one who offers God praise but it also impacts the lives of others. These psalms also reveal God's greatest desire for his children is for them to desire him and his will for their lives. They teach that while believers should not live in the past, they must never forget it. Remembering God's faithfulness in the past gives believers strength to trust the Lord in the present and future. Finally, believers must recognize difficulties are a part of life in a fallen world. We are either going into a trial, in the midst of a trial, or coming out of one, but God is always faithful and near.

# Hope in God

*Psalms 42–43*

## The Big Picture

Book II of the collection of the psalms begins with Psalms 42–43. Most scholars believe that the two originally were one composition and that perhaps for liturgical reasons they were separated into two separate psalms later. Indications they were originally one psalm are as follows: Psalm 43 has no heading to separate it from Psalm 42, many Hebrew manuscripts combine Psalms 42–43 into one psalm, the two psalms share the same refrain, "Put your hope in God, for I will still praise him" (42:5, 11; 43:5), and both share similar phrasing. The author and specific occasion of Psalms 42–43 is unknown. However, they are the laments of one who against his will was a great distance away from the house of God and the people of God and longed to be back with them as he contended with the taunts of his enemies. His prayer was for God to vindicate him and return him to the temple. Even though his situation appeared desperate, his resolute faith led him to hope in God.

## Digging In

The heading of these psalms indicate they are a "maskil," a psalm of instruction meant to enlighten those who hear or read it. Psalms 42–43 reveal how people who trust in God can be enlightened when thoughts of despair have darkened their perspective. The "sons of Korah" were worship leaders in the temple who used this composition to minister to the people of God.

In Psalm 42:1–5, the psalmist expresses his longing to be with the people of God worshiping the Lord in his temple. He begins by comparing his deep yearning for God with the severe thirst of a deer that is desperate for water during a time of drought. He thirsts for "the living God," who, unlike the impotent false gods of the nations, is able to answer his prayer. The psalmist's desire for God consumes him, and he will not be satisfied until he can return and worship God at the temple, the place of God's manifest presence (v. 2).

It is during this time of isolation from the people of God and the temple that the psalmist's enemies taunt him, questioning the existence of the psalmist's God saying, "Where is your God" (v. 3). It painfully grieves the psalmist as a feeling of abandonment by God apparently begins to play on his mind (see v. 5 and 43:2). The psalmist is heartbroken as he reminisces the times he was the first in line leading many of the people of God to the house of God with joy and thanksgiving. At the same time, these memories remind him of the joy and the profound sense of gratitude one experiences when one directs one's devotion and faith toward God. His memory also reminds the psalmist that although he is alone and surrounded by unbelievers, there is encouragement in knowing he is not alone in his faith in God (v. 4).

Consequently, the psalmist rebukes himself for his sense of despair. Then, he follows his rebuke with an exhortation, "Put your hope in God!" together with a declaration, "I will still praise him, my Savior and my God." To hope in God is to wait expectantly for him to act. When the psalmist looks to God, it is then that he sees the One who is his salvation (v. 5).

In verses 6–11, the psalmist recognizes his depression and the added oppression of his enemies. Nevertheless, he also knows the only remedy for his problems is the Lord. Instead of being in Jerusalem at the temple, the psalmist was in a region a little over one hundred miles to the north. Therefore, although he is not where he would like to be, he will focus on the Lord where he is (v. 6). The headwaters of the Jordan River contain rushing water and waterfalls crashing down from the slopes of Mount Hermon. The psalmist uses this picture to describe the precarious state in which God has put him. He is barely able to keep his head above water (v. 7). Nevertheless, he recognizes God's faithful love for him at all times and therefore will sing a song of prayer to God in his darkest hour even though he wonders why God has allowed him to go on suffering the way he has (vv. 8–9). Moreover, the psalmist's enemies continue to taunt him by questioning God's faithfulness and ability to save him, crushing his spirit (v. 10). So the psalmist repeats to himself his rebuke, his exhortation, and his declaration that he uttered in verse 5 (v. 11).

In Psalm 43, the psalmist continues to combat his discouraged perspective with prayerful words of affirmation of God's faithfulness and ability to protect and save him. He prays God will silence the repeated taunts of his deceitful and unjust enemies and that God would publicly vindicate the psalmist's faith in God (v. 1). Then emphatically, the psalmist declares God is his refuge. But this is his perplexing difficulty. Since God is his refuge, why has God apparently rejected him and allowed him to continue to suffer (v. 2)?

The psalmist realizes he will get his answer when he returns to God's "holy mountain," Mount Zion is where God's temple resides. The psalmist's desire has not changed. He prays that God will give him his "light" and "truth" to lead him back to Jerusalem. *Light* often refers to salvation and "truth" to God's faithfulness to his Word. He knows God is his salvation and faithful to keep his promises (v. 3). Therefore, he anticipates the joy of worshiping at the altar of his one and only God (v. 4). The psalmist emphatically concludes in verse 5 with his repeated refrain, speaking words of truth to himself: *Don't be discouraged! Hope in God! Continue to praise your Savior and God because when you think about it, you will always have reason to do so!*

## Living It Out

Sometimes there are times when God leads us through barren seasons in life in order to renew our appetite for him and the fellowship of other believers. God's desire for every believer is to delight in him. It is easy to take for granted the blessing of worshiping with the people of God in the house of God until we are separated from them. Let us never take for granted such wonderful gifts and opportunities from God. Poorly attended houses of worship and joyless worshipers who do attend indicate a loss of appetite to enjoy the Lord and the privilege of being part of his people, joining them in celebratory worship of our Lord. When our tears have been our food day and night and it is difficult to sense God's presence, we must put our hope in God by recalling all he has done for us, we must praise the one who has saved us and look to the light of his truth to lead us.

# The Suffering of the Faithful

*Psalm 44*

## The Big Picture

Like the heading of Psalm 42, Psalm 44 is also "A Maskil of the sons of Korah." The psalm describes a time in Israel's history when its army suffered a sound defeat in battle, but it gives no explicit indication of when the battle happened or who it was that defeated Israel. It best fits a time before the exile when the people were loyal to God. For instance, there were surely many temporary setbacks when David led his army against their enemies. The writer of Psalm 44 appears to have been the king or at least a representative of the king. He is especially distraught and perplexed because even though the nation has been faithful to Yahweh, the Lord apparently has forsaken them and caused them to suffer defeat and humiliation before the nations. God did not answer their prayers for victory as they prepared for battle. Therefore, Psalm 44 is a national lament, complaining to God for rejecting Israel and choosing to ignore their prayers. Nevertheless, the psalmist continues to trust in God as he concludes the psalm with an earnest plea for Yahweh to "wake up" and help his people.

## Digging In

Psalm 44 begins with the psalmist acknowledging God's great works of salvation and victory on behalf of the nation of Israel in its past (vv. 1–3). Serving as a reminder, the psalmist gives an account of how the people of his day have heard the stories from their ancestors, stories passed down from one generation to the next, concerning all that God had accomplished for them. In particular, the psalmist refers to the conquest of the land of Canaan when God went before his people and displaced the Canaanite nations and settled the Israelites in the Promised Land (vv. 2–3). The psalmist emphasizes that even though Joshua and the Israelites fought against the Canaanites, there was no question that God gave Israel their victories. Their total victory over the stronghold at Jericho is an example of this truth (Josh. 5:13–6:27). God did all of this through his might, "your right hand, your arm," and his favor, "the light of your face" (Ps. 44:3), on his people, Israel (Deut. 7:7–11). The people have not forgotten what God had done.

In Psalm 44:4–8, the psalmist declares his confidence in God's ability to also give Israel victory over their enemies now. He proclaims God is his "King." The one who rules over the psalmist is the one he trusts and serves as he submits to God's sovereign will. The psalmist recognizes God is the only one who decides if Israel will win its battles (v. 4). The psalmist believes the promises God made to his ancestors to fight for his people and give them victory in his power are still true (vv. 5, 7). Furthermore, the psalmist wisely recognizes that his weapons of war are useless without God's intervention. It echoes Proverbs 21:31 which states, "A horse is prepared for the day of battle, but victory belongs to the Lord." He declares their faith in God to help them now in Psalm 44:8 by Israel's boasting "in God all day long." They already take great pride in their God and in what he has already done. What's more, they recognize their indebtedness to God for all he has already done. As a result, their intent is to praise his name "forever."

The words "But you" in verse 9 turn attention to the heart of Psalm 44 as verses 9–16 describe the grievous situation the people of God are experiencing. The psalmist's candidness and accusing tone is startling as he directly addresses God. He begins by blaming God for what has happened by saying "you have rejected and humiliated us." You caused us to suffer defeat and therefore to retreat from our enemies. God, you are the reason they were able to plunder our possessions. You are the cause of the deaths of so many of us as we were slaughtered "like sheep." You are the one who has sold your people for nothing to be deported into slavery. And you are the one who has made your people a "laughingstock" and an object of "ridicule" among the nations. Consequently, the demoralized psalmist laments the humiliation he suffers as he repeats one description after another of the contempt he and his people suffer. The people of God have become a reproach, a source of mockery and ridicule, a joke, a laughingstock, a disgrace, and a picture of shame all because God did not intervene on their behalf.

Nevertheless, with all that has happened the people of God still have "not forgotten" God or "betrayed" God's covenant. That is, they have continued in their faithful obedience and devotion to God (vv. 17–18). While this is true, it appears God has treated them as if they have been unfaithful. To "crush" in "a haunt of jackals" and to "cover" with "deepest darkness" means God has put them in a desolate place looming with death (v. 19). The psalmist's question in verses 20–21 recognizes God's omniscience. If the people had been unfaithful, God would know. Verse 22 is the key to the message of Psalm 44. It is not because of their unfaithfulness to God but rather because of their faith in God that they are like flawless sheep that have been sacrificed to him. Loyalty to God means willingly laying one's life down for him even unto death.

Psalm 44 concludes with a desperate cry to God to take action and save his helpless and defeated people. The reason God should redeem them is because of his "faithful love," his *ḥesed*. The psalmist knows God is faithful to the covenant promises he has made to Israel. While the psalmist fails to understand God's actions, he knows he can trust in God's character.

## Living It Out

God will use his people to bring glory to himself not only in times of abundance but also through times of suffering. Our faithfulness to God as we endure suffering and ridicule for our faith is a glorious picture of the Lord Jesus Christ. Even our Savior cried out to God to remove the cup of suffering he would endure, but because of the joy set before him, our salvation and the will of his heavenly Father, he gladly went to the cross (Mark 14:36; Luke 22:42; John 18:11; Heb. 2:9–10; 12:2). [The apostle Paul quoted Psalm 44:22 to encourage believers who were suffering persecution (Rom. 8:36), and he expressed a desire to know the fellowship of Christ's sufferings (Phil. 3:10).] Like the Lord Jesus Christ, believers may expect undeserved suffering before experiencing the full delight of God's blessing. [Our desire should be to glorify Christ with our lives in whatever way he wills as we anticipate the joy to come.]

# A Royal
# Wedding Song

*Psalm 45*

## The Big Picture

Psalm 45 is a wedding song apparently sung by a royal court official celebrating the union between a mighty Israelite king and his beautiful bride, most likely the daughter of a foreign king for the establishment of an alliance between the two kingdoms. It is difficult to recognize to which particular king this psalm refers, but its recognition of the king's close relationship to God suggests a godly king like David or one from the Davidic line. Ultimately, it foreshadows the Messiah, the Lord Jesus Christ and his bride, the church. After the introduction in verse 1, the psalm praises the king in verses 2–9. After that, in verses 10–15 the psalm turns its attention to the bride, giving her royal counsel as she assumes her new position as queen. The psalm concludes with promises of perpetuity and praise for the king (vv. 16–17).

## Digging In

The heading of this psalm has the notation, "according to "The Lilies" which also occurs in the headings of Psalms 69 and 80. "The Lilies" is probably the title of the musical arrangement to which the words of this psalm were supposed to be sung. The phrase, "a love song," indicates the intent of the psalm as it celebrates the love that the king and his bride share for one another. Furthermore, like Psalms 42–44, this psalm is a *"Maskil,"* a psalm of contemplation, to be utilized by the temple's worship leaders in congregational singing.

The psalmist's introduction in verse 1 reveals to whom and for whom the psalm was written, the reason for writing the psalm, and how it was written. Since 2 Timothy 3:16–17 indicates all Scripture is God-breathed, inspired by the Holy Spirit, this psalm was written to and for "the king." Certainly, it was written for a particular king during Israel's history. However, the heightened language of the psalm led several Jewish rabbis to understand the king to whom this psalm was written is the Messiah.[3] *Messiah* means "anointed one" in Hebrew. *Christ* means "anointed one" in Greek. Therefore, when the New Testament writers referred to Jesus as the Christ, they were declaring Jesus is the Messiah. So as we read this psalm we may think of the Holy Spirit speaking to its original context while at the same time anticipating its supreme meaning to be found in the Lord Jesus Christ.

The reason the psalm was written was because the psalmist was unable to retain the abundant warmth he felt for his good and excellent king, which was "a noble theme." This psalm came from the "heart." However, it was not just an emotional outburst or mindless babble. Instead, it was the eloquent product of the psalmist's endeavor to thoughtfully construct and convey his admiration of his king with maximum effort and meticulous precision (v. 1b).

The psalmist began his focus on the king in verses 2–9 by describing how God has eternally blessed the king, declaring he is the most extraordinary man to ever live. Of particular remarkableness was the graciousness of his speech. In Isaiah, the Servant of the Lord, the Messiah, said, "The Lord GOD has given me the tongue of those who are instructed to know how to sustain the weary with a word"

(Isa. 50:4). Furthermore, when Jesus returned to Nazareth and taught in the synagogue, those who heard him "were amazed by the gracious words that came from his mouth" (Luke 4:22).

The psalmist affirmed the king was awesome in majesty, a mighty warrior equipped to press ahead and fight victoriously in the cause of "truth, humility, and justice." The psalmist is sure the king will do so with mighty "awe-inspiring acts" that strike fear in their enemies and produce a profound awe in his people as no enemy can stand before him (Ps. 45:4–5). Moreover, the king's throne is established forever. The Israelites did not believe their kings were divine. Calling the king "God" in verse 6 denotes the close relationship this human king, who the psalmist served, had with God.

However, in light of the person and work of Jesus Christ, the fulfillment of David's eternal throne is altogether accomplished by Christ. The writer of Hebrews quotes verses 6–7 and affirms the king who fulfills Psalm 45 is Jesus (Heb. 1:8–9). Because he was characterized by a love for "righteousness" and his complete rejection of "wickedness," God has given the king joy, and his greatest joy was the bride who is adorned in the rarest and finest gold who stood at his "right hand," the place of greatest honor (Ps. 45:9). This picture anticipates the church, the bride of Christ, made up of every believer, in all its beauty and splendor as the inhabitants of a New Jerusalem (Eph. 5:25–27; Rev. 21:9–11).

In Psalm 45:10–15, the psalmist turned his attention to the bride. The psalmist advised the bride to sever past allegiances and pledge her wholehearted respect and devotion to the king. Doing so, the bride will be fittingly attractive to her husband. However, as a result of her commitment to her king, he will not be the only one who recognizes her. The nations also will recognize her exalted position and seek her favor (see Rev. 21:24–26). What is more, the bride will celebrate and rejoice in the presence of her king.

Psalm 45 concludes with a declaration of the king's perpetuity; he will have blessed offspring for generations and the king's name will be remembered for generations (v. 16). Given the final parallel statement that the nations will praise the king's name forever, the "generations" of verse 16 should be understood to continue for eternity. In other words, the children of the king will live forever and sing his praises eternally (v. 17).

## Living It Out

Psalm 45 teaches that just as the psalmist was circumspect and attentive in what he wrote, there is a place for thoughtful and attentive expressions of worship. Certainly, we often respond to God with extemporaneous expressions of joy. However, it is also good to give some thought to expressing our praise to the Lord. Therefore, we can learn how to express our worship of King Jesus from the psalmist's example. This psalm should also remind us that we must not only be mindful of our words to God but also of our words to others. We are like Jesus when the words we speak are gracious to those who hear them. Furthermore, we should learn to appreciate as best we can just how impressive our Savior is. Finally, as believers in Christ and members of his church, the bride of Christ, we need to heed the psalmist's advice to the bride and desire to be attractive to Christ by our submissive, wholehearted devotion to him.

# God Our Refuge and Strength

*Psalm 46*

## The Big Picture

Psalm 46 communicates a deep trust in God in the face of overwhelming threats. It begins with the voice of man and concludes with the voice of God. It is impossible to be sure of the occasion that precipitated the writing of this psalm. Nevertheless, the Assyrian attack led by Sennacherib against Jerusalem is a strong possibility. King Hezekiah and the inhabitants of Jerusalem faced what appeared to be an unwinnable situation. However, the Lord saved the people of Jerusalem as he alone utterly devastated and defeated the Assyrians, killing 185,000 of them in one night and causing the rest to flee (2 Kings 18:13–19:37). It appears to be such an untenable situation that gave rise to the writing of this psalm.

Psalm 46 has a straightforward structure of three sections, each set apart by the word *Selah* The meaning of *Selah* is unclear. The Hebrew root appears to mean to lift up, so it could mean raise the volume. Some suggest it indicates a musical pause, and others believe it serves a structural purpose to divide the various sections in the psalms. Sometimes

these divisions in the psalms are less obvious than in others, but in
Psalm 46, *Selah* appears to serve the purpose of division. In Psalm 46,
verses 1–3 emphasize how God's presence shows he is more powerful than all the forces of his creation. Verses 4–7 indicate that God is
present with his people and protects them, and verses 8–11 reveal that
God's presence with his people guarantees the defeat of their enemies.

## Digging In

As we have seen in the headings of other psalms, Psalm 46 was
to be led by the sons of Korah, the worship leaders at the temple. The
word *Alamoth* refers to young women of marriageable age and could be
the name of the tune that went with the psalm or perhaps that young
women had a major role in singing the song in worship.

Psalm 46 begins with a strong declaration of confidence in God.
When the people of God face insurmountable difficulties of life, they
can find shelter from the onslaught in him. God is the one to run to
because he alone is *our refuge*. Additionally, God is our *strength*. He
enables his people safely to weather the storms of life. What's more,
God's help is not just a contribution. He helps abundantly because his
people will always find him in times of need since he resides in them
and therefore is always with them (v. 1). He will thoroughly meet their
needs by assisting them and doing for them what they are helpless to
do for themselves.

Because it is God who is the abundant helper of his people, they
have no reason to fear the most powerful threats on the earth. He is
the Creator. He is omnipotent. Even when it seems like our world is
falling apart, is chaotic, and out of our control, when the landscape
around us suddenly shifts and there appears to be no firm foundation,
the people of God have no reason to fear. In the ancient Near East,
mountains were places where people fled to take refuge from the threat
of their enemies (e.g., Gen. 19:17; Josh. 2:16; Ps. 11:1). Accordingly, the
psalmist is saying that even when all the other places of security and
refuge may disappear like mountains toppling into the depths of the
terrifying, chaotic sea, we can trust in God to protect us and save us
(Ps. 46:2–3). The people of God are secure in him.

The city of God is Jerusalem, the place of God's manifest presence to Israel, but there appears to be no river flowing through the city. The Hebrew word that is translated *river* in verse 4 also means "stream" or "current." For this reason, this "river" should be understood as the Gihon Spring that flows underneath the city of Jerusalem. Since the city's existence, it has supplied Jerusalem's inhabitants with an ample supply of water even when surrounded by enemies and laid under siege. In ancient times, cutting off the water supply to a city under siege was a key strategy its assailants used to make it surrender. Typically, people cannot survive more than three or four days without water. The psalmist recognizes that because God provided his life-giving and sustaining water to the inhabitants of the city of God, they would not perish (v. 4). Ultimately, the city will not fall because the Lord himself is within her. His presence alone is enough to defeat their enemies. The darkness of despair turns to joyous morning when the people of God recognize that God is their help. His enemies melt in fear before him. Accompanied by his heavenly hosts, the LORD is with his people, and he is a towering stronghold for his people that is unassailable by their enemies (vv. 5–7).

Verses 8–11 emphasize these truths. Just as the people of Jerusalem must have looked in amazement over the walls of Jerusalem as they witnessed the decimation God wreaked on Sennacherib's army when God slew 185,000 aggressors against his people, the psalmist invites his people to witness how God has saved them. The weapons of the enemies were shattered and their supplies were consumed with fire. When God fights for his people, their enemies suffer a total defeat and his people relish the experience of total victory (vv. 8–9). It is futile to fight against God. Wisdom would be for God's enemies to surrender to him, to know that he is God and to worship and exalt him. This is God's merciful and gracious invitation to all people from every nation. If they would do this, they too could sing the psalmist's concluding refrain, "The LORD of Armies is with us; the God of Jacob is our stronghold" (vv. 10–11).

## Living It Out

Christians should be the most fearless people on the face of the earth. If we would only recognize the profound truth that God is our refuge and strength who is always ready to help us in our most dire times of crisis, then not only would we be at peace but we would also communicate the wonderful salvation we have in Christ to a lost world. Furthermore, we must realize the futility of fighting against God and his will for our lives. It is when we seek to know him and worship him that we may experience his wonderful presence and unshakable protection in life.

# Sing Praise to Our King

*Psalm 47*

## The Big Picture

Psalm 47 appears to be a continuation of Psalm 46. In Psalm 46, we saw how the psalmist invited his audience to "Come, see the works of the Lord, who brings devastation to the earth" (46:8). One can imagine the picture of the people of Jerusalem looking over the city walls and witnessing the decimation as God poured out his wrath on the menacing Assyrian invaders who were threatening to raze the city. An explosion of rejoicing replaced their foreboding sense of fear and dread when the city's inhabitants realized God had saved them. Psalm 47 is the expression of their joy and gratitude as they praise God for being "King over the whole earth." The initial writing of this psalm seems to have happened in response to such a victory over the enemies of the people of God. Its structure is 1) a call to praise God for what he has done (vv. 1–4), 2) a call to recognize his sovereignty over all the earth (vv. 5–7), and 3) a call to recognize God's sovereignty over the nations (vv. 8–9).

## Digging In

The psalm begins in verse 1 calling all the "peoples" to praise God. "Peoples," "nations" and "the whole earth" demonstrate that people from every nation must recognize who God is and praise him. There is a prophetic ring to this summons because David and the prophets foretell there will be a day when people from every nation will worship the Lord (e.g., Ps. 86:9; Isa. 49:6; 66:18–21; cf. Rev. 5:9–10). Equally notable is the manner in which the psalmist calls the peoples to worship. He implores them to "clap your hands" and "shout to God with a jubilant cry." The clapping of hands and shouts of jubilation are expressions of celebration, appreciation, and victory (e.g., Ps. 98:4–8). It is the natural response of a people who recognize the gravity of the hopeless situation they were in and the marvel of the salvation they have experienced by the hand of God.

Verses 2–4 give reasons the peoples should praise the Lord with such enthusiasm. First, as "the Most High" and "King over the whole earth" the Lord is "awe-inspiring." The pagan gods of the nations are nothing compared to him because the Lord alone is "Most High." Consequently, since the Lord is "King over the whole earth," in awe of the magnitude of his majesty, everyone should bow to his sovereign rule. Verse 3 declares another reason for praising the Lord is because he brings the enemies of his people under their submission just as is described in Psalm 46:9–10 when God silenced their enemies. Moreover, God gave the land of Israel and the city of Jerusalem to his people as their inheritance from him. The enemies of the people of God cannot take away the precious and priceless inheritance God has given his children. Why not? Because the people of God are his pride and joy. He loves them (Ps. 47:4). Therefore, he will not allow it.

Verses 5–7 depict God ascending in the midst of "shouts of joy" and the "sound of trumpets." To where is he ascending? Verse 8 states "God is seated on his holy throne." It could refer to a victory procession to the temple since the ark of the covenant in the Holy of Holies represented the holy throne of God. Its lid was called the mercy seat. It was from there that God said he would speak concerning the Israelites

(Exod. 25:17–22). The psalmist calls the people to praise the king and sing a song of wisdom, an enlightened song of recognition.

Like above, these verses have a prophetic aspect to them as they anticipate the ascension of the Lord Jesus Christ to his heavenly throne once he had conquered sin and death, the enemies of his people, through his crucifixion and resurrection from the dead. In his short one-verse record of Jesus' ascension, Luke does not mention any shouts or trumpets, but it is clear that the biblical writers do not record every detail of every event (Act 1:9). However, the men in white clothes who addressed the disciples at his ascension said Jesus will return "in the same way you have seen him going into heaven" (Acts 1:11). Concerning Jesus' return, Paul writes, "For the Lord himself will descend from heaven with a shout, with the archangel's voice, and with the trumpet of God" (1 Thess. 4:16). It follows, if this is the way Jesus will return, then it is the way he ascended. Perhaps the shout and blowing trumpets at Jesus' ascension were only heard in heaven. Regardless, when the Lord Jesus Christ ascended into heaven, he took his place on his rightful throne (Rev. 3:21).

As the previous verses have shown recognition of God's sovereign rule over the whole earth in general, Psalm 47:8–9 recognizes God's sovereignty over the nations in particular. They answer to him. His throne is holy because God alone rules over the nations. No human power compares to him, and every seat of human authority comes from him (v. 8). Furthermore, the psalm concludes with another prophetic picture: people from the nations assembled as part of the people of God, belonging to God and bringing glory to him (v. 9).

## Living It Out

When believers come together to praise the Lord, it is appropriate to express enthusiastic celebration and appreciation for the victory they have in Christ. The anemic and pathetic way some sing "Victory in Jesus" conveys a much louder message than the words coming out of their mouths. Through Christ Jesus' sacrifice on the cross, God has defeated our enemies, the world, the flesh, the devil, sin and death, and what is going on now is a "mop-up operation." In the present, God enables us through the work of the Holy Spirit to defeat our enemies, but it is an ongoing struggle for us. However, the day is coming when these enemies of the people of God will be once and for all eliminated. No one can take away the inheritance of the abundant and eternal life we have in Christ because we are his pride and joy and he loves us. Because of him, we have a wonderful future. We should pause and think about these truths and then exuberantly sing praises to our Savior and King.

# Behold the God of Zion

*Psalm 48*

## The Big Picture

Psalm 48 is the third of three consecutive psalms that commemorate God's defense of Jerusalem, the city of Zion, and the utter defeat of its enemies. While these psalms do not explicitly mention Sennacherib's invasion of Judah, his encirclement of Jerusalem, or God's decimation of his armies in 701 BC as recorded in 2 Kings 19, this significant and extraordinary victory God won for the holy city of Zion best fits the occasion for the writing of these psalms, and it is possible that Isaiah or Hezekiah was the author. Psalm 46 describes the immediate aftermath of God's victory, describing what God had done and how the people initially responded with jubilant amazement. Psalm 47 recalls the victory procession to the temple as Yahweh ascended to his throne in the Holy of Holies. This concluding psalm of the trilogy is a hymn of praise for what God did and for his manifest presence in Zion with his people. The structure of Psalm 48 is as follows: verses 1–3 are a call to praise God in recognition of who he is; verses 4–8 describe how the Lord defeated the arrogant enemies of Zion; verses 9–11 extol the

Lord for his faithful love and righteous judgments; and verses 12–14 are the psalmist's recognition of God's gracious deliverance as a pledge of God's eternal faithfulness to his people.

## Digging In

Verses 1–3 are a timely reminder that it is good to recognize God's greatness and praise him for it. In these verses, the psalmist recognizes God's greatness as he manifests it in the presence of his people in Jerusalem, the city of Zion. It is there in his holy temple he shows that he is with his people. As God has saved his people from the threats of their enemies, the people of God realized that God's presence with them meant they had no need to fear their enemies. It is similar to what Isaiah said to the Assyrians when they invaded the holy land: "Devise a plan; it will fail. Make a prediction; it will not happen. For God is with us" (Isa. 8:10).

Moreover, God's presence on Mount Zion makes it the "joy of the whole earth" even if the whole earth fails to realize it at the time. The only hope for salvation for the nations is in God's salvation and in no other. Mount Zaphon is a mountain north of Zion and was believed by the Canaanites to have been the abode of their patron God, El (Ps. 48:2). Nevertheless, the God in Zion is the most High God and his presence on Mount Zion makes it the greatest of all mountains. It is not the height of Mount Zion that makes it splendid, but it is God who makes his presence known there that makes it splendid. Furthermore, the walls and citadels of the city are not nearly as impressive as is God himself who is the true "stronghold" of the city of Zion (v. 3). Even though their enemies said they could not trust in the Lord, the people of Zion trusted in God and the Lord vindicated their trust in him (see 2 Kings 18:19–35).

Psalm 48:4–8 describe what happened when Zion's enemies advanced against the city. A number of vassal kings loyal to Sennacherib joined the Assyrians in their advance to assault Jerusalem (v. 4). However, what they saw froze them with fear. It was not the city of Jerusalem and its man-made defenses that caused it. These were seasoned conquerors who had brought down cities much bigger and better fortified than what Jerusalem was. What caused the "trembling" and "agony like that of a woman in labor" was the "stronghold" of Zion, God himself (vv. 5–6). Like a strong wind destroying ships of Tarshish, the most impressive ships of that time, God crushed these enemies (v. 7). The power of God to save his city and its inhabitants was no longer hearsay to the people of Zion because they witnessed him defend his city with their own eyes. God will make sure his city and his people are established "forever" (v. 8).

The natural response to witnessing and experiencing God's extraordinary deliverance is to praise him for what he has done. Verses 9–11 depict the psalmist doing this in the temple first by contemplating God's faithful love, which is grounded in his covenant with his people. God is committed to his people. What God does on behalf of his people serves as a witness to the nations as to who he is. Therefore, news of God's saving his people spreads, and just as his renown reaches the ends of the earth, so does his praise. The people of God are glad and rejoice because God uses his power to do what is right for his people and defeat their enemies (v. 11).

Finally, the psalmist concludes by encouraging the people to take note of what God has done so that they can pass it down to future generations (vv. 12–14). He tells them to go around Zion and observe how the enemy failed to touch the city. Its towers, ramparts, and citadels were in the same pristine condition after the enemy's invasion as they were before. God's protection of them was as complete as the defeat of their would-be assailants. Therefore, the witnesses of such a great salvation must tell their children what God has done because he is their eternal God. Those who trust in God can depend on him always to lead them.

## Living It Out

Just as the psalmist recognized God's greatness because of his manifested presence with his people in the temple, so believers today can praise God because he has made us temples of his Holy Spirit and he resides in us and will never forsake us. We have no reason to fear when the Lord is our stronghold. The Lord Jesus Christ has defeated our most menacing enemies, so there is no reason to fear them. We can rejoice in knowing that God is eternally committed to his children; we are secure in him. Additionally, we should contemplate how much God loves us, what he has done to demonstrate his love for us and tell others how he has saved us. We can have confidence in our God, assured that he will always do what is right for us, keep us, and lead us until the day we die and on into eternity.

# The Futility of Trusting in Material Wealth

*Psalm 49*

## The Big Picture

Psalm 49 is a wisdom psalm. The wisdom literature provides instruction in practical living for those who are devoted to God. It does so by contrasting a life lived foolishly with a life lived wisely. By explaining what it means to fear the Lord and by dealing with the ambiguities of life, questions arise indicating what we know is right according to God's Word appears to contradict what we perceive to be happening in the world. Psalm 49 addresses one of these ambiguities: Why do people who trust in themselves and their achievements often appear to prosper while those who trust in the Lord often struggle throughout their lives? Or, is a worldly life really a futile life and a life lived for God truly a blessed life? Typical of wisdom literature, verses 1–4 give a universal call for all to listen to this wise instruction. Verses 5–9 indicate that no amount of money can pay God to keep one from dying. Verses 10–12 recognize the temporariness of wealth and the certainty of death. Verses 13–15 reveal that those who trust in their wealth and those who trust in God have two very different destinies.

Finally, verses 16–20 encourage believers not to fear the rich and ruthless because their end is sure.

## Digging In

One of the characteristics of wisdom literature is its universal audience. Therefore, the psalmist in Psalm 49 begins with a call to all people everywhere to hear and listen to what he is about to say. However, verse 2 indicates how he wants to address them and anticipates what his focus of concern is. Also, its parallelism reveals who is at the center of his attention. The psalmist employs a common parallel structure common to Hebrew literature called a chiasm. Here it is an A-B-B-A structure where the first two ideas or words are repeated in reverse order with the second two ideas or words. The first two ideas, "low and high," are repeated in reverse order with "rich and poor." "Low" and "poor" correspond to each other and "high" and "rich" correspond to each other. Furthermore, the idea in the center (B-B) is the writer's most emphasized idea. In this case, the psalmist indicates the "high" and "rich" will receive his main attention, while at the same time the psalm provides instruction everyone else needs to hear.

In verse 3, the psalmist states that he will speak wisdom, and those who carefully study what he teaches will gain understanding. But what is wisdom in the Bible? Wisdom has four dimensions in the Bible. 1) Wisdom can refer to a skill such as a potter has in his craft. 2) Wisdom may also refer to being shrewd or crafty. Or, 3) wisdom can refer to applied knowledge, the ability to practically and skillfully navigate through everyday life. However, as the psalm progresses, we will see what the psalmist has in mind, 4) wisdom is instruction that comes from God and ultimately leads one to God. It is theological. Here, God is both the source and goal of wisdom. The answer to life's most profound and perplexing questions come from him in his Word. Additionally, the psalmist has put this wise instruction, this proverb, to a song so that it will be easily recalled as music often stimulates memory.

In verses 5–6, the psalmist clearly communicates his concern is about those who "trust in their wealth and boast of the abundant riches." He is not saying being wealthy is sinful. There are plenty of people in the Bible whom God blessed with tremendous material wealth who were faithfully devoted to the Lord such as Abraham and Job to name a couple. However, those who fail to acknowledge God as their true source of blessing and have the audacity to take credit for what he has done are the psalmist's focus. They often despise the upright and use their money and power to treat believers with contempt. However, those devoted to the Lord have no reason to fear those who disdain them.

In Old Testament law, there were instances when a person could pay a sum of money called a ransom instead of offering a sacrifice, thus saving the life of what was supposed to be put to death. Nevertheless, verses 7–9 indicate that no amount of money will be enough for a person to pay God for the price of eternal life. It is a hopeless pursuit.

Why? Because death is certain for everyone, the "wise" and the "foolish." Furthermore, we all come into this world bringing nothing with us and likewise every one of us departs this world leaving all behind. Everything we accumulate in this life will end up with someone else (v. 10). The only permanent home for the "arrogant," those who put their trust in themselves and their wealth, is a grave no matter how renowned and respected they were before they died (vv. 11–13). Death will lead them like a shepherd to Sheol, the place where the dead reside and bodies decompose. In contrast, God will do for the upright what mere humans cannot do for themselves. He will redeem those who trust in him, save them from the power of death, take them, and receive them to himself (vv. 14–15).

Psalm 49 concludes by directing our attention back to the issue the psalmist called his audience to contemplate. Those devoted to God need not fear the abuse of those with wealth and power no matter how arrogant and dominant they may be while on this earth because their days are numbered. What's more, it is foolish to envy them. They may congratulate themselves for their accomplishments and receive the acclaim of others, but their time is short. It will all come to a permanent end. Just as multitudes like them have perished, they will also perish. The person who fails to understand and embrace the wisdom that comes from God and leads to faith in God will in the end have lived a futile life (vv. 16–20).

## Living It Out

This psalm has a similar message to John 3:16: "For God loved the world in this way: He gave his one and only Son, so that everyone who believes in him will not perish but have eternal life." Everyone has a choice to either trust in themselves and their own judgment and accomplishments or to trust in God for salvation. The inheritance of those who arrogantly trust in their own accomplishments is to perish, but the inheritance of every person who has placed his or her faith in the Lord Jesus Christ is eternal life because God has paid the ransom and redeemed every believer with the blood of his Son. Believers must not envy those who will soon *lose* everything when in Christ we eternally *have* everything. Instead, let us rejoice in our Redeemer.

# God's Courtroom

*Psalm 50*

## The Big Picture

[Psalm 50 is prophetic in nature because much like various passages in the Prophets, it depicts God's convening a trial in his own courtroom—bringing charges against his own people, Israel.] It is a poetic vision that vividly depicts God's accusations and judgment concerning his people's failure to worship him the right way. The structure of this psalm is straightforward: verses 1–6 depict God accompanied by a devouring fire and raging storm summoning heaven and earth to gather his faithful ones to face him in court; verses 7–15 reveal the first of two accusations God brings against his people; verses 16–21 reveal the second of these two accusations; and verses 22–23 contain parting words of warning to those who disregard God's instruction and blessing to those who devote themselves to live according to God's Word.

## Digging In

The psalm begins with a magnificent description of God's "perfection of beauty" and brilliant "radiance" as he summons the heavens and the earth to gather his people to face him in court (v. 2). The names of God reveal who this God is who is summoning his people to face his judgment (v. 1). First, he is "the Mighty One, God," indicating that God has the ability to execute judgment. Unlike the false gods of the nations who are nonexistent and whose words are therefore empty, the Mighty God has the power to do what he says he will do. Additionally, he is "God," Elohim, the Creator of the heavens and the earth and all that are in them. His awesome ominous power is on display as he comes with devouring fire before him and a raging storm all around him (v .3).

Second, in Deuteronomy 10:14 Moses declared, "The heavens, indeed the highest heavens, belong to the LORD your God, as does the earth and everything in it." Consequently, God not only has the power to carry out his judgment concerning his people but he also has the authority to do so since everything and everyone ultimately belongs to him, the Creator. Third, this God who is summoning Israel is the "LORD," Yahweh, their personal covenant God. The charges the Lord is about to bring are personal offenses that have harmed Israel's intimate relationship with him. Expressions throughout the psalm such as, "our God," "my faithful ones," "those who made covenant with me," "my people," and "your God" all demonstrate the personal nature of Yahweh's charges against his people.

God summons the whole earth to witness what he is about to do with his people. All will witness that "he will not be silent." God will confront this people who had made a covenant with him at Mount Sinai to be completely devoted to him but now have broken their promise. Yahweh has found his "faithful ones" unfaithful. All of creation will see God's justice carried out even on his own people, and the heavens will declare that God does what is right as "the Judge" (Ps. 50:6).

Before God delivers his first accusation against Israel, he explains the basis for doing so: you are "my people" and "I am God, your God" (v. 7). This word is to believers. The first accusation pertains to their worship through offering sacrifices to God. However, it is not because they have been negligent in this. It appears that they were doing what the law instructed them to do in regard to the stipulations of when and how to offer sacrifices (v. 8). The problem is not with what they were doing in worship but with their motives as they offered their sacrifices.

They had the notion that somehow God "needed" them to offer sacrifices to him. In the ancient Near East, people commonly believed the sacrifices they offered to their gods served the purpose of feeding their hungry gods. This erroneous thinking appears to have seeped into the thinking of the people of Israel concerning the one and only true God, Yahweh. Therefore, God's message is clear: "I don't *need* you. I am not dependent on you." Every animal in the forest, all the cattle in every pasture, every bird and every creature belongs to God. God does not get hungry, but if he did, he would not need anyone to provide food for him. God is self-sufficient; he needs no one's help for anything (vv. 9–13).

Instead of thinking that they could help out a "needy" God, the people of Israel needed to recognize their dependence on him. A "thank offering" was a way of showing recognition of what God had done to meet the needs of his people by offering to him thanksgiving and praise. Expressions of gratitude and praise would serve to remind them that it is not God who needs them but that they desperately need God. They will honor him when they recognize their helplessness and trust in his salvation (vv. 14–15).

Verses 16–21 reveal God's second accusation against his people: hypocrisy. They recited his Word and claimed that they were devoted to God, but their actions contradicted what they said. Their words of devotion unaccompanied by faithful obedience were empty and revealed an inauthentic love and commitment to God. They paid lip service to God's Word while at the same time rejecting it. They were comfortable with profiting from the underhanded activities of others. These unfaithful people to God were comfortable with associating with those who were unfaithful to their spouses to the point of accepting and condoning such behavior. Furthermore, these people sought to harm others with their tongues by deceitfully slandering them, even their own brothers. While all of this happened, the Lord patiently kept silent. Consequently, these hypocrites mistook God's silence as approval, thinking God was just like them. However, they could not have been further from the truth. God will confront and rebuke them for their sin.

The concluding two verses of Psalm 50 contain a warning and a promise. Those who fail to repent and choose to disregard God and his Word will be punished, without exception. Because they have rejected the Savior, when his judgment comes, they will have no one to save them. In contrast, those who demonstrate their faith and total dependence on God by offering him thank offerings and living in such a way that demonstrates evidence of their faith in God will experience his salvation.

## Living It Out

Our erroneous conceptions of God can lead to greatly offending God even if we are convinced we are faithfully worshiping and serving him. Therefore, it is of utmost importance that we seek to know God through his Word and guard ourselves against the world's notions about God that can corrupt our understanding of him and what he expects of his children. Psalm 50 teaches that God is most honored when believers recognize their helplessness and need of God. Jesus said, "You can do nothing without me" (John 15:5). The Lord receives glory through our weakness. Therefore, we must recognize how our praising of God acknowledges our need and be ever mindful that he is all we need. Finally, we must live in such a way that honors God. It is an expression of our love for him. Moreover, our obedience to God's Word does not earn us eternal life, but it points others to the Savior who by grace through faith has already saved us. Such obedience demonstrates how God has met our greatest need through his Son, the Lord Jesus Christ.

# *Notes*

1. "About How Many Stars Are in Space?" UCSB ScienceLine, https://scienceline.ucsb.edu/getkey.php?key=3775, accessed May 7, 2019.

2. See the comments concerning a "Maskil" and "the sons of Korah" at the beginning of "Digging In" section on Day 33.

3. See http://oneinmessiah.net/Psalm45Messiah.htm (accessed September 6, 2019).

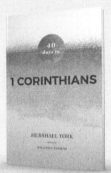